DEC 6 1982

Dear Norma,

Thought this book would fill in your spare time with a subject matter you truly love—poetry. Your so gifted in this area, your name should also be included with "New American Poets."

Love & Best Wishes to you all

Your ol' friend Helen

1644 So. 63 St.
Milwaukee, Wi, 53214

P.S. I like P.34 "I carried with me Poems"
P.145 "Unending Sameness
of Questionable Quality"

31 NEW AMERICAN POETS

American Century Series

HILL AND WANG | NEW YORK

31 New American Poets

Edited and with an Introduction
by Ron Schreiber

Foreword by Denise Levertov

Manufactured in the United States of America
234567890

ACKNOWLEDGMENTS

The editor is especially grateful to the poets themselves for permission to publish their poems. Many of the poems in this volume were originally published in magazines; some appeared in books by the individual poets. Grateful acknowledgment is made to the following:

Apple, for John Stevens Wade's 'The Ascent,'

Duke University *Archive*, for Alex Raybin's 'Dream' and 'Titan's Lament.'

Aspen Poetry-Prose Workshop, for Ethel Livingston's 'Unending sameness of questionable quality.'

Beloit Poetry Journal, for Dave Etter's 'Country Graveyard' and 'Prairie Summer' and Phyllis Harris' 'The Source.'

Boss, for Clive Matson's 'Vision: Second Psalm.'

The Canadian Forum, for John Gill's 'Frances.'

Centering, for Sister Mary Norbert Körte's 'The Poets of Peace and Gladness.'

Chelsea, for Jack Anderson's 'Habitat' and 'The Invention of New Jersey,' copyright, *Chelsea*, 1967, and John Haines' 'The Stone Harp,' 'The Cauliflower,' and 'The Color,' copyright, *Chelsea*, 1968.

Choice, for Jack Anderson's 'A Dream of Metals.'

Colorado State Review, for Keith Wilson's 'The Streets of San Miguel.'

El Corno Emplumado, for Keith Wilson's 'Old Love.'

Depauw Magazine, for John Gill's ' "Today Well, Tomorrow Cold in the Mouth." '

Descant, for John Stevens Wade's 'Jigsaw.'

Down Here, for Clive Matson's 'Against Jealousy.'

Duende Press, for Keith Wilson's 'Old Love,' from *The Detroit-Albuquerque Family: Seven Poets*.

dust, for Gene Fowler's 'The Words' and 'Shaman Songs' 2, 10, and 12.

dustbooks, for Gene Fowler's 'The Words' and '305 Honda' from Gene Fowler's *Field Studies*, copyright, 1965, dustbooks, and Gene Fowler's 'Shaman Songs,' 2, 10, and 12, from Gene Fowler's, *Shaman Songs*, copyright, 1967, dustbooks. Reprinted by permission of dustbooks.

The Minority of One, for Dan Georgakas' 'As soon as he learned' and 'Hiroshima Crewman.' Reprinted by permission of *The Minority of One*.

University of Missouri Press, for Nancy Willard's 'The Church,' 'Crewel,' and 'In Brittany,' from Nancy Willard, *Skin of Grace*, copyright, 1967. Reprinted by permission of University of Missouri Press.

The Nation, for Jack Anderson's 'Night, Window, Wind'; Robert Hershon's 'Report to the Blue Guard'; Dick Lourie's ' "english," '; Jason Miller's '(Square in Savannah)'; and John Stevens Wade's 'Jimmy's Father' and 'Ticktacktoe.' Reprinted by permission of *The Nation*.

University of Nebraska Press, for Dave Etter's 'Prairie Summer,' from Dave Etter, *Go Read the River*, copyright, University of Nebraska Press, 1966. Reprinted by permission of University of Nebraska Press.

NEW: American and Canadian Poetry, for Jim Harrison's 'Night in Boston,' Robert Hershon's 'Paintings of Roses,' and Dick Lourie's 'Two Birthday Poems.'

NEW/BOOKS, for John Gill's ' "Today Well, Tomorrow Cold in the Mouth," ' 'Conjured,' and 'the other garden,' from *Young Man's Letter*, copyright, John Gill, 1967; and Robert Hershon's 'In This Forest,' 'Report to the Blue Guard,' 'The Shoemaker's Booth,' 'We Are,' 'The Zoo Club,' 'Child at Sand,' 'Midtown Poem,' 'On Horror,' 'German Eyes,' 'Loves of the Public Servants,' and 'After,' from *Swans Loving Bears Burning The Melting Deer*, copyright, Robert Hershon, 1967.

New University Thought, for Jim Harrison's 'War Suite.'

Niagara Frontier Review, for Clive Matson's 'Drink Wine in the Corner Store.'

Nightshade, for Victor Contoski's 'Inscription on an Altar of the Dead' and 'Keepsake.'

One Two One, for G Bishop's 'Pissarro's one pure note.'

The Open Letter, for Besmilr Brigham's 'tomb.'

Out of Sight, for Victor Contoski's 'Autumn.'

Oyez Press, for Gail Dusenbery's 'I carried with me poems,' 'The Backyard on Fulton Street,' 'New Year's,' 'Midnight on March 27th,' 'Letter to Duncan,' 'The Guitar,' 'The Shadow,' 'Saturday Night,' and 'The Opening Session of Congress Rock and Roll,' from *The Mark*, copyright, Gail Dusenbery, 1967. Reprinted by permission of Oyez Press. Also for Sister Mary Norbert Körte's 'To Dance in a Loving Ring,' ' "a new flower—pure and untorn," ' 'That Is Tad,' and 'The Poets of

Symptom, for Besmilr Brigham's 'the will's love.'

Synapse, for Doug Palmer's 'In a field.'

Synapse Press, for Doug Palmer's 'My people,' 'In a field,' 'High Tide, and,' 'Clap hands,' and 'These poems,' from Doug Palmer, *The Quick and the Quiet*, copyright 1965, Doug Palmer.

University of Tampa *Poetry Review*, for Victor Contoski's 'Fallen Tree Elegy' and John Unterecker's 'Rain Portrait.'

things, for Dick Lourie's 'The WhenIwas,' 'The Bestfriend,' 'The Madman Looks at His Fortune,' and 'The Madman Goes to a Party.'

Tri-Quarterly, for Dave Etter's 'Firewood Hill' and Robert Hershon's 'Midtown Poem' and 'On Horror.' Reprinted by permission of *Tri-Quarterly*.

Unicorn, for John Haines' 'The Great Society' and 'It Must All Be Done Over....'

The University Review, for Nancy Willard's 'I Knew a Boy Who Ran with the Dogs.' Reprinted by permission of *The University Review*.

Vassar Review, for Nancy Willard's 'Crewel.'

West Coast Review, for John Gill's 'poem.'

Wild Dog, for Gene Fowler's '305 Honda' and Keith Wilson's 'The Horses.'

The World, for Joel Sloman's 'Blueprint.'

The Yale Review, for John Unterecker's 'Fish,' copyright 1967, Yale University. Reprinted by permission of *The Yale Review*.

I'm writing this foreword on trust, having before me only the list of poets to be included in the anthology, not the poems themselves. That seems a foolish, even an irresponsible, thing to do. It requires an explanation:

First, I know the work of a good many of them already, and care about it: a few are former students of mine. Second, my own experience (as a former poetry editor, for some years, at *The Nation*, and recently as compiler of an anthology for the War Resisters League 1968 Calendar; as well as having been the recipient, in recent years, of uncounted numbers of manuscripts from young poets, sent sometimes for criticism, sometimes just to state their existence) has caused me to know how much remarkably good poetry is being written in America at this time; and I feel a reasonable assurance that Ron Schreiber, though undoubtedly he will have accepted some work I would not have chosen, and though he has omitted the work of some poets I wish he had included, will have assembled here a collection that will give to readers hitherto unaware of what is going on among the young poets some idea of the variety and fertility of the work that is being done.

The fact that writers, most of them in their twenties (a few older, but some even younger), are thus fertile and are writing in general on such a high level at such a time in history—a time when we are all *living at war*, a time of shame and fear and of extreme uncertainty about the future—seems to me very important. Their generation is making it increasingly clear that it has a radically different sense of what human life should be from that of its parents and grandparents: a sense expressed roughly in the slogan Make Love Not War. That slogan does not merely stand for the debatable issues of a sexual revolution but for a humane and positive desire to live and let others live abundantly—not merely to "co-exist" but to *live* together: an intention akin to Schweitzer's concept of Reverence for Life ("I am life that wants to live, among other forms of life that want to live")—whether they have read him or not. Never before in history have there been so many people who rejected, as not only abhorrent but bizarre, the very idea of war as a solution to anything; and who are able to make the connection between war and profit. This is a generation which does not want to make a lot of money in order to buy a lot of *things*. It doesn't go for that kind of success. And though it is always only a small section of any generation that formulates and demonstrates new feeling, yet this different sense of life is present in many, many more than in those who are able to articulate it. No matter what these poems are "about," there is a relation between their being written at all and that obstinate and beautiful desire to live.

The very fact that so much poetry is being written and that so much of it is good represents, then, in this darkness in which middle-aged poets like myself often feel discouraged and futile, something very moving, something of hope and energy, which more people ought to know about. That is why I am going out on a limb to write a foreword to an anthology I have not read.

DENISE LEVERTOV

CONTENTS

The first thing to say about American poetry today is that there is a great deal of it and that a surprisingly large number of poems are very good. While most English poetry, whatever its imagery, sounds very much like English poetry written fifty years ago, much American poetry sounds like something new, as if "free verse" had been tamed into cadences.

It was not difficult to find thirty-one poets to fill a new anthology. Among the manuscripts I had before me when I made this selection were the works of nearly fifty poets who consistently write good poems. I arbitrarily excluded everyone who had been represented in two earlier anthologies of new American poetry—Donald Allen's *The New American Poetry* and Paris Leary and Robert Kelly's *A Controversy of Poets*. I also excluded accomplished poets—such as Michael O'Brien, editor of *The Eventorium Muse*—who work primarily in traditional forms and metrics. Since I made these selections, I have come to know the work of other good poets—such as Floyce Alexander, Hale Chatfield, Sam Cornish, Luis Garcia, and Margaret Randall—of which I had previously been ignorant. This anthology is, however, representative of a vigor and variety characteristic of American poetry today.

Dramatists and novelists sometimes are financially richly rewarded. Few poets, however, have illusions about the nature of their success. No one in this country will get rich by writing poems. Only a few in fact can even make a living from writing poems—and that comes only after many years and indirectly: through fees for readings sometimes, but usually by occasional grants or by academic positions sometimes set aside for better-known poets. Of the poets here, only five or six are university teachers, and only one, to my knowledge, Jim Harrison, holds an academic position because he is a poet. Some are housewives, one is a teaching Dominican sister, at least one is still a student, two work as editors, one owns a coffeehouse, one sings songs for children, one—Doug Palmer, under the name Facino—writes poems for passersby in San Francisco, some pick up work as best they can. They are all professional poets. They write poems, as any poet does, because they have to and want to. Wide recognition is often late in coming—seven of these poets are over forty—and commercial success is usually reserved for other genres.

But commercial success often carries its own binds; formulae for selling tickets or getting magazine serialization or book club distribution can be exceedingly restrictive. Denied the rewards of commercial success, a poet is also likely to be free from its limitations. If it is difficult for him to become widely known, a poet is at least likely to see his poems produced. Established poetry magazines such as *Poetry, Beloit Poetry Journal,* and *Poetry Northwest* are not confined to poets of wide reputation. Other magazines—like *Evergreen Review, Hudson Review, The Nation, Quarterly Review of Literature,* and *Paris Review*—publish good poems by relatively unknown poets. And many presses—university presses like Wesleyan, Yale, Missouri, and Nebraska, and commercial presses like Doubleday, Grove, and Norton—are printing books by young poets. The most common place of publication for good poets without wide reputation, however, is the little magazines whose circulation is usually under a thousand. The reader who cares about good poems will find them consistently in *El Corno Emplumado, Grande Ronde Review, Hanging Loose, kayak, Mimeo, NEW: American and Canadian Poetry, Potpourri,* and University of Tampa *Poetry Review.* These and other small poetry magazines are edited by poets. They are unsubsidized, sometimes mimeographed, often irregular in publication. They are often ephemeral as well; LeRoi Jones' *yugen,* a regular place of publication for what has since become a whole generation of widely-known poets, is no longer published. Some of these magazines are also occasional presses. Gene Fowler's first books are dustbooks; the first books of Robert Hershon and John Gill are published by NEW/BOOKS; *kayak* has brought out handsome volumes by many good poets. Other small presses—Journeyman Books in Brooklyn,

Oyez Press in Berkeley, The Poets Press in New York—often specialize in books of poetry.

I recently read an article about M. L. Rosenthal's *The New Poets* in which a reviewer spoke confidently of the critic's vital function as an intermediary between the poet and his potential audience. The reviewer seemed to think that without the critic most poets would be inaccessible to readers or listeners. In fact he is exactly wrong. Rosenthal has helped readers to see what they may previously have missed in many poets, and he has been especially useful in introducing good poets to wider audiences, as when he introduced the poems of William Carlos Williams to responsive young Germans.

But most young poets need no special critical introductions. The magazines in which their poems appear are usually magazines of poetry, containing little or no criticism. And many poets who are not widely known are nevertheless widely published.

They are also widely heard. G Bishop's poems often seemed dense to me when I first encountered them on the page; when I heard the poet read in a New York coffeehouse it became clear that the way he sets down his poems on the page is a guide to reading them aloud. Extra spaces between words invariably indicate pauses. *All* his lines are end-stopped, even those that end with prepositions or articles. Other poets in this anthology use similar conventions of spacing. Jack Anderson, John Haines, Emmett Jarrett, Dick Lourie, Jason Miller, Joel Sloman, and John Stevens Wade use similar conventions of end-stopped lines. Some poets do not punctuate at the end of a line, feeling that the line-end itself is sufficient direction to pause.

If one hears a poet read—and ideally this or any other anthology would include records of poets reading—the poet's rhythms are clear, and good poetry now, as most good poetry of the past, is meant to be read aloud. Many young poets are experienced readers. Throughout the country they have read on college campuses and in coffeehouses. In San Francisco poetry readings have been presented in conjunction with folk or rock concerts. New York poets read during the Week of the Angry Arts and long after on a "poets' caravan" that traveled on an open truck through the city. Boston poets read to support the Resistance. Poets who read in New York public schools frequently found that the most direct responses to their poems came from students in vocational high schools, who had not been trained to explicate and analyze. When a poet reads, there is no critic present to mediate between a poet and his audience; their relationship is direct.

What has happened is that the poets themselves have become direct. And their directness is not primarily a matter of content or tone but a matter of form, especially of rhythms. There are still competent poets who write odes and sonnets in rhymed iambic measures, but the trouble with old forms and rhythms—as Ezra Pound noted a half-century ago—is that they have already been perfected.

Metrical poetry—that is, poetry that can be scanned according to a two-stress system—is based upon the counterpoint between the metrical rhythm (iambic, anapestic, trochaic) and the way in which a poem is actually spoken. No one, after all, actually speaks iambics or ever did; among other things, there are more than two degrees of stress in both English and American speech. But one familiar with the great poems of the English language hears the contrast—the almost infinite number of variations—between the meter and the spoken poem, and he finds that contrast pleasing. But now we have grown used to these meters; they no longer excite us or even necessarily keep us alert. Much modern metrical verse seems to have been written for classroom study. And the poet who writes such verse is likely to be restricted as well in what he sees—his vision can scarcely be larger than the form in which he expresses it. The most exciting metrical verse being written today is the lyrics of songwriters (John Lennon and Bob Dylan, for example). It is not spoken but sung; it is based upon a different contrast—that between the metric and new musical rhythms.

The rhythms in which these poets write are not metrical at all. They are based upon phrases of American speech exactly as older verse has been based upon a metrical norm. A phrase of speech is simply a group of words bounded by pauses and usually containing—on a scale of four stresses rather than the two stresses of metrical scansion—only one primary stress. The speech phrase is only the *basis* for a poet's measure; because of the way in which he sets down his lines, it may contrast with the way a poem is actually read.

One can hear the measures easily when he hears a poet read his own poems, but not everyone lives in a large city or near a college campus where readings frequently take place. There are, fortunately, other guides: many poets, for example, pause at the end of each printed line. Each of the first three lines of Victor Contoski's "Grief" is a separate measure:

> When I was introduced to Grief
> I was prepared for anything
> but the joy-buzzer in his hand.

In these lines and in the following lines by Jack Anderson, the printed line coincides exactly with the speech phrase:

> Place a custard stand in a garden
> or in place of a custard stand
> place a tumbled-down custard stand

The lines of Emmett Jarrett's "Runes" are longer. Sometimes one must simply take a deeper breath to read the whole line, though punctuation within the line of course indicates pauses:

> I picked up six black stones on the beach today,
> put them still damp in my pocket and brought them home
> to play with,
> forgot them for a while, eating supper, then remembered
> and took them out, dry now, to look at.

Instead of normal punctuation, some poets use spaces within a line to indicate pauses. Dick Lourie pauses at the end of each printed line, often where one would not think to pause in normal speech, but he also pauses when a phrase ends within a line:

> this morning   though I had heard about him
> from my friends I saw for the first time the
> Hitler Dwarf   whistling and striding up to
> me through the dirty snow piles alongside
> Seventh Avenue   the short solid legs
> slightly bent   the familiar mustache a
> brown trenchcoat almost to the ground   he said

Clive Matson writes in longer groups of phrases, clearly indicated by indentation and spacing between lines:

> Today
>   another irresistible force,
>   have to swing with it.
>   Heavy clouds &
> I wait for the tables to turn
>
>   or push it a little,

Robert Lax uses even larger spaces between lines and stanzas. What looks at first like a concern for typography or appearance on the page is in fact directions to the reader telling him precisely how long to pause.

Usually a poet writing nonmetrical verse helps the reader to hear his rhythms by the way he sets down his poem on the page. Sometimes, however, the poet writes neither by the line nor by the stanza. These lines from Marge Piercy's "Apologies" do not telegraph their rhythms:

> Moments
> when I care about nothing
> except an apple:
> red as a mapletree
> satin and speckled
> tart and winey.

There is obviously no two-stress metric in these lines, and the reader who knows how to speak his own American idiom should have little trouble reading them. The first three lines can be read, just as they would normally be spoken, without pause; the last three lines each form a separate phrase or measure.

But Americans speak differently from one another. Because they base their rhythms in a common principle does not mean that poets write or sound alike. In fact, if I have chosen well, each poet in this anthology sounds unlike every other poet. His voice, though grounded in a common measure, is unique. (On the contrary, poets writing metrical verse often do tend to sound like one another.)

For many of these poets—as for Robert Creeley, Robert Duncan, and Denise Levertov—the measure has to do with the printed line. Dick Lourie counts syllables to determine the length of his lines; Emmett Jarrett does not. Joel Sloman's long lines, resembling those of Whitman and Ginsberg, seem to be composed of separate phrases; so are John Unterecker's long lines, but his rhythms are not like Sloman's. Marge Piercy's measures often run from line to line; so do Besmilr Brigham's, but her measures seem to stem from a condensed, sometimes gnarled syntax, and they are usually shorter than Piercy's. I hear Doug Palmer's short lines as separate measures each, but his syntactical units are longer, and one can hear different, but equally sure, rhythms if he measures Palmer's poems by grammatical phrases.

I've talked about the measures of nonmetrical verse because I think that the introduction of measures based upon speech phrases is the most important technical innovation in twentieth-century American poetry. But a technical innovation means little in itself. What critics have called "free verse," implying that many poems have no discernible form or measure, might better be called "direct verse." Direct verse is free not in the sense that it is unstructured but in the sense that directness and freedom from traditional forms and measures have enabled poets to see freshly; their vision has expanded.

In his essay "Projective Verse" Charles Olson pointed out

that the form of a poem properly follows its content. It has been put another way: that there should be no artificial forms into which the poet must fit his expression but only forms organic to particular poems. Many poets still adhering to old forms, some of whom are widely known and widely studied, tend to pad—to include extra words or syllables to fill out their measures. Such a habit can lead to myopia and even dishonesty. Their verse has become, I think, increasingly urbane and private.

What is happening with direct verse is a continual discovery of new forms. And new forms are important because the form of a poem is the vehicle for its content. As forms expand, so does the vision of poets.

Today our poets and musicians have become our best seers. And we need them. Our politicians are intelligent only when they listen to men and women many years their juniors. Most of our university presidents and generals are totally mired in old forms; they don't listen at all, and they've gone blind.

Well, the poets here are worth listening to, not just for the ways they sound but because they see clearly. Most of the poets in this anthology write love poems well, and many of them write poems that explicitly condemn a society where love falters and war thrives. Some are frankly and unselfconsciously religious, and all have found those places where the spirit can exult or rage. Some have begun again to write long poems; others are poets of the macrocosm in short, clean lines. The flowering of new poetic forms has been a simultaneous flowering of vision.

Here are thirty-one American poets. They know their craft well. If you will forget preconceptions and listen attentively, you can hear their songs. And if you will watch attentively and open yourselves to receive their words, you will see a clear and powerful light.

RON SCHREIBER

JACK ANDERSON

Habitat

1

Greasy water   surely polluted by this time
the heavy throbbing like monstrous sex
from the tracks   freight cars boxcars coal cars
refrigerator cars gondola cars   repeated   freight
        cars boxcars coal cars
    repeated across the horizon
    row after row of tractors
    (each one the same)
    goes by   boring
boring   do kids still spend
summer evenings down by the grade
watching, counting the cars   throwing a stone?
smoking maybe   We are born here. I
was born here, near here   where you can hear the
        drop forge
when the wind is right.

2

Simple, almost elegant   water towers
how their thrust refreshes the attention
from the monotone of trains   still, over that way,
        smoke stacks
not just one   a whole line, tubular
like empty toilet paper spools, like the way they wrap
piles of change at a bank, like—
    —like nothing but what they are
      and in a hurry
        —the stacks
—smoke stacks spew such black clouds of smoke
there is nothing else to think about, only one thing to do:
    women run screaming into their kitchens
    to shut the windows quick.

Wherever they walk, grit crackles underfoot—
some shrug   a few nervous ones have hysterics

("Honey, no one likes it, no one does")

3

I sit at a table   with a shudder
I remember I   I do not know what mustard is
or how they make it   (I start losing control
in my own kitchen)   I know nothing, I do not know
how they make a pickle.
And salt? Well, the ocean is salt (yes, go on):
and Great Salt Lake and the Dead Sea   but
how do they get it out of the sea?
     (I can think of several ways they might, for example—
                         —The point is
I don't know.
I don't know what happens either
     when I turn on the light switch
     when I turn on the faucet
     when I telephone you babbling wildly and hear you
tell me you learned all this in fifth grade.

Homework: 1. Light a fire without matches.
               2. Wire a five-story apartment house.
               3. Diagnose the diseases of sheep.
               4. Build a screw propeller.
               5. Milk a cow.
               6. Fix the plumbing.

Cranes (birds?)stretch   cranes stretch across factory
                                   yards / they
are not birds / they are as strange
coal rattles down the chute   brakes squeal
I take off my coat, wipe the sweat from
my eyes   I keep jamming the gum machines.

My one cure for anything
is to shake it up   or kick it.
I watch the sky being irrigated with streams of black smoke.
I know nothing about all this.
I have never known anything else.

The Invention of New Jersey

Place a custard stand in a garden
or in place of a custard stand
    place a tumbled-down custard stand
in place of a tumbled-down custard stand
    place miniature golf in a garden
    and an advertisement for miniature golf
        shaped for no apparent reason
        like an old Dutch windmill
in place of a swamp
    place a swamp

                or a pizzeria called the Tower of Pizza
                    sporting a scale model
                        of the Tower of Pisa
                or a water tower resembling
                    a roll-on deodorant
                or a Dixie Cup factory
                    with a giant metal Dixie Cup on the
                                                    roof

In place of wolverines, rabbits, or melons
    place a vulcanizing plant
in place of a deer
    place an iron deer
    at a lawn furniture store
    selling iron deer
        Negro jockeys
        Bavarian gnomes

and imitation grottoes
with electric Infants of Prague
in place of phosphorescence
of marshy ground at night
place smears of rubbish fires
in place of brown water with minnows
place brown water

gigantic landlords
in the doorways of apartment houses
which look like auto showrooms
auto showrooms which look like diners
diners which look like motels
motels which look like plastic chair
covers
plastic chair covers which look like
plastic table covers which look like
plastic bags
the mad scientist of Secaucus
invents a plastic cover
to cover the lawn
with millions of perforations
for the grass to poke through

In place of the straight lines of grasses
place the straight lines of gantries
in place of lights in the window
place lighted refineries
in place of a river
place the road like a slim pair of pants
set to dry beside a neon frankfurter
in place of New Jersey
place a plastic New Jersey

on weekends a guy has nothing to do
except drive around in a convertible

counting the shoe stores
and thinking of screwing
his date beside him
a faintly bilious look
perpetually on her face

Night, Window, Wind

All night long the window
kept blowing open
bringing the last of the rain
to my pillow

letting the light deepen
along the ceiling
and the curtains run loose in
mild disorder

each time it blew open
I would awaken
to fasten the window but
it would not stay

again it would open
before I could sleep
until the morning grew wide
with thoughts of sleep

but the light seemed lighter
then than anywhere
and oh how the air was sweet
after the rain

Winter Twilight

The sky looks half-erased,
washed out.

On a park bench in the shadow
a woman sits
plucking the hair from her head.
Then she unrolls her face
the way she might unroll a stocking.
Only the head itself is left—
white
blank
an egg.
She leans back,
breaks the egg against the bench.

Now darkness can begin,
and soot, and plunder.

The Rendezvous

She waits in a white dress
holding flowers of white snow

But he has come from the mines
without stopping to wash

So he runs away and hides
and hopes on his return that

The dress will be soiled
the flowers melted

But when he comes back
the flowers have multiplied

The dress stands clean and rigid
and she has vanished completely

A Dream of Metals

It was then I dreamed
of small metal objects
tacks to secure
casters to run on

I sorted locks, hooks
bolts and brads
staples loaded in a staple gun

I fill a bureau drawer
with clamps, valves
little wheels, springs
of no known source
or use
which nag to be used

on which I cut myself
and my blood tastes
of copper, silver, and tin

It was then I dreamed
of small metal objects

hinges like cocoons
on the sides of doors
screws thirsty for wood
the hibernation of spikes
on the roadbed

The small metals
trembling as though magnetized

rise one by one
out of the houses they hold together
out of the girders
out of the floorboards
out of the wings of tables

rise up in a cloud / merging
returned to their ore in mid-air
while the cities below them
fall like folded paper

clips, iron filings
the fillings of teeth
sawteeth, tenpenny nails
nuts, pins, and cogs
the strips around the lids of coffee cans

ascending transfigured
like small angels toward the sun

G BISHOP-DUBJINSKY

Pissarro's one pure note

For Stuart

decide   on   a   sound

not ice:cubes on my knee
(a summer place
 in the country)

noise to listen for
a rustling:unresolved
hopefully),

or the silence   heard/

neither every word,
clay in the ear,
                    a tempo:touch
                       breathing,pace
                       star:light/

 fetchingly, my eye:lids
she grabs my tongue

  slides it into   cunt:/
not pitch,tone— the shade
(of yellowness)

:encircle   the   sound

not to carve   (texture:
the day recounts the birds,
a photograph of wind
:an intrusion

               anticipated:sudden
:a manner of hearing:

you (her eyes, solstice)

you (her eyes, solstice)
whisper deliberately
the sun has dimmed

/i was gone

the postcard from the south
said   you were warm
that the wind at night
was cool   (windows open:

   a week ago the day
   was absolute zero

1 will not meet you),
it is snow silent
& i am north of your words:

direction is not surface(
the moons are wrapped
in wool)

i see your hair

you (her eyes, equinox

Alice 1963

—for Warren and Jane

"I shall sit here," the Footman said,
"on and off, for days and days."
—ALICE IN WONDERLAND

six   seven   6, 7

The syncopation of the clock
changed
when the finely veined hand
moved
near the maroon cat.

There in that painting
    6, seven   6   7
is the same detail of the room:
mirror   up & down the wall
a silver bowl of fruit
the leather chair   where
the old squire
and his black Cheshire   had sat.

shafts of dusk
the stained glass

chalkier light   than before.

my daily melon
—for Susan

very ripe today.
outside it looks like honeydew; inside, cantaloupe.
im not sure what kind it is.

i puff on a cigar...

the garden grows everyday. it grows up and grows down.
it grows sideways too.

a typewriter is handy. i'll type something:
    my tongue is taking a bath. come back later.

a lazy day.

my cat reads Endymion, very slowly.

you
enter this space that i reserve for my daily melon:

NOW

the yellowpink butterflies
from Egypt
skim the flowers
and fly over the dune to the sea.

they have traveled
months of days
(through powdery moonbeams)
to be here
when the flowers die.

the yellowgreen butterflies
from Egypt
are jewels of eyes—
stones of the rainbow.

is here, as if

light through the window
(unassuming, delicate):
                              the walls:
        patterns of flowerheads   (a child face)
falling into place,   dreams.

the sound of silent movies/ the projector:the screen/
—sounds that our eyes relate to us
        (as if a child screamed).

                a geometry of words curls from lips:
    'time   is a passing that lasts',
        mathematics fails us   (:pinpoint bombing).

we proceed

to discuss the average age
that artists have died
(dead children die young).

                        the projector continues

unraveling the film
...i see my face melting

onto my chest, you
watch my feet for movement
(inter/relation you thought important:

say anything
& i will relate it to something else
de rigueur is mentioned)

you say heart.

quellisma,
seven variations.*

(*from a longer poem in many parts:*
"Distance Away/Space Between")

amber eyed girls continue to stand   naked
between the dusty mirror and the candycase.

                                                                (shields

of night—
              replica, figment
the room smells of dried bones)

she stands   a bunsen burner
                      hourglass
                      powdered poison.

   ***

     yellowtailed sparrows
wait misty-eyed on the ledge.   lights flicker on

* quellisma *means a yearning, a keening, a crying-out for something; it
describes the wailing of flamenco dancers.*

& off
      (ripped sheets slide from the window
onto mosaic flowerheads, oriental screens sway back

& forth churning the air).
metalic butterflies fly from the wall
                              (they collide
in the third dimension   sparkling as they disintegrate

forming clusters of roses).

***

the amber eyes dangle in the darkness

***

      onionwhite solitude hushes the stars
we listen for silence but we hear nothing

:she is asleep dreaming of sleep, she breathes
 to the rain tempo, the venetian blinds filter
 light across her face.

***

      goldtoothed women grin in chorus,
      waiting for their lovers.

      they dance, dresses of sunlight
      glint as they sway—

                  the rhythms
      of receding shadows are music enough.

***

the matches
in the icebox
mysteriously lite
melting the milkcartons.

***

dawn.   she turns her head
        in the direction of Persia.

        chalk circles revolve
        & expand.

        the silent nearly
        silent chant of snow.

        she remembers the symetry of emptiness.

        she sips coffee, gazes out the window.

ancient maps are spread on the table (maps
        possibly from Egyptian tombs tracing
        the route of the sacred cats on their
        journey from Thebes to Ptolemy's room)

the moon
        changes color with her mood. today
        it is ochre   yesterday it was azure.

she sits as she has been sitting:

***

tell our daughters

each is beautiful
a woman's life
makes it (that awareness)
through her touch

      descendants
of strict age
set against vanity

not secure in loveliness

a girl is born
like a little bird opening its wing
she lifts her face
in a down of feathers

a rose
   opens its leaves
with such a natural care
that we give words for
petal deep
in the imagination

                a word becomes
                a bitter thing
                or a word is
                an imagination

tell our daughters   they are
fragile as a bird
strong as the rose
deep as a word

and let them make
their own growing time

                big with tenderness

The Carver and the Rock Are One
(as we are one who move upon it)

(debt to Nahuatl)

Looking into the man god's stone
made with featured movements /living
shapes carved out by tool and hand
from some known face
                wearing a war helmet

the arch bow of the lips thick with speech
that stays so, as though a breath stopped him
wide nostrils full of air
              and the sudden, expanded
eyes—pupils looking beyond wood's growth

where the head, separated from the body,
lies fallen; its countenance intent.

There is something he cannot tell us!
And the mind feels back for that direction—
of who made him, whose hand
upon that slightly spread mouth. Just open
to size that little birds might have nested there,
or in the under-curve nostril.

Wash chips in the solid unbroken rock
weather wearings
from under-earth seepage
              where he
in stone patience . . .
waited an eternity for disinterment.

And now he will live again—sheltered
behind red velvet drapery cloth, returned

a king (as he was once), his bodiless head placed
on a square block throne in his country's museum.
Silent before his own people, the drawn-long
blood of their descendants.

                And though the mouth
never opens, and the eyes never close,—
a live face can without deceit
get caught up into it, the breathless stoppage
held in that arch

whirled to the eyes with their unmoving stare.

ii

            the body
            (if ever there was one)
            bore itself a stone heart

yet the heart says to the heart:
There is nothing after.

Life rests in the flesh—

Hold to my stilled face and know.
I carried in my hand stones and a battle axe
inset with knives of obsidian
that my power moved with to see men die;
and that I live now . . . it is only in your
imagination. My own life passed from me
by way of a man stronger at that moment
than I was. By grace the carver so kept this
helmet on. It was not an humiliation.

            the great pupils startle
            open with what the dead saw

<pre>
                    (why do you
hold down shut your own dead's eyes)
</pre>

        . . . there is nothing beyond. And all
glory, as all grace—you with your legends!
strange to me as mine are strange:
we fulfill ourselves (of and from and) upon
this earth. And all after is the grave.

The round discs of the stone
stare—as the living
look up into them and stare.
The eyes say to the eyes:
Past flesh—no god can save you.
                              All things
die with their sights empty.

"When my enemy struck his blade,
I was not stone. The earth has healed . . ."

The Crosses

About these column faces
a row of stones
has become a horse trough

pigs
root under the ramada
whose foundation
men
        of the bright murals made

generation of conquerors
who built over deep earth forms
a mosaic of man

in these dry mountains
—or high plains

where the atmosphere
holds hard against destructive
roots
to make use of . . .

distinct civilizations that passed—
one of the square tree cross
the other a man-body shape

And a man goes on using—:
the hard-stem cacti for wall
cathedral cactus boundaries
against his inner cathedral

high stiff cane
and marsh tul-e grass
the mashed stone
calcium
bone-rock brought up from the rivers
and he put up his
own brief shelter

like wanderers moved in
thick as blown mesquite beans
plaster against rock
quick hard mud
     a house!   a house to live in
     over the old kings' walk

A mud-dauber
has taken over the sweet honey hive

a pig skin bloated with pulque
now hangs beside the conqueror's door

the ghosts of the dead

                                        hover about us
walkers in darkness—
or an inhuman light
old men and old women with long white hair

beasts that fought in the fields /plains
shadows through woods and wide sky places
animal masks on their faces
bears   wolves
in bloody steps of the minotaur
crying at night
gaunt creatures with matted fur and hair

saints making their own cross vision
high above a white world covered in snow
they carry a holy stick
and intricate kind ways
to tear a lone man's heart out calling
                                god   god
the passionate renunciation
great bare walkers our fathers
looking for Atlantis
travelling for a ninth sky heaven their naked bones
heaved from the earth they rejected
maniacs riding their own skeletons with long manes

and day dancers
those who lay by the streams happy for bread
for love for joy
cherishers of flesh
heavy fools who did not want much the clowns
—

ghosts of the dead that call out and stalk through us
through our uncertainty
walkers in darkness
and we human of light

answer and feed on them drowning in

                                    war   —or god
god of war
let us sit down awhile and be still

like strange animals strange to one another
and strange to the earth

tomb

bone to bone
the bodies wait

crunched up
thrown from the sky
caged in nakedness

a jar of stones big as the moon
since their sun's turning

white
bone-writing
laid out in form
that sleeping children take
facing one another

bare
fallen cold through flesh
fierce rocks that once made

                        a generative light

the will's love

love God—
         my mother said
He who shut the Lion's mouth
and sealed the flames to their own burning

"the soul is like a little bird in His hand
a bird that lives in a wild briar tree"

love Life—my father said
laying the map out
         green-red mountains
         blue-yellow sea
the soul is a migrant
roe-bird that nests on sea rocks
a hawk   a falcon—
                 an eagle
or a "splatter-wing parrot
that only at night sleeps in a tree"

it took
my childhood before I could see

each one
said the same
         I am

             love me

VICTOR CONTOSKI

The First Animal

The first animal
lives under my house.

When I sleep
it comes through the wall,
settles its bulk on my chest,
and puts its lips to mine.

It eats my breath.
When I die it will starve.

Keepsake

I keep a pair of lovers in my pocket,
shrunk and mummified according to
traditional rhythmic incantations.

No bat wing or mandrake root for me.
They say my stuff has good seasoning
with just the old, reliable lovers.

And yet I can't help thinking of late
they've lost the early flavor, being
perhaps too long without light and

having the unpoetic company of greasy
coins, buttons, and snotty handkerchiefs.
Someday I'll have to get rid of them

for a fresher pair with more juice,
but I'm a sentimentalist unabashed.
I like the homey feel of old lovers

jouncing together there in the dark
like nickels, all their rough edges
removed. Souvenirs of the war.

Money

At first it will seem tame,
willing to be domesticated.

It will nest
in your pocket
or curl up in a corner
reciting softly to itself
the names of the presidents.

It will delight your friends,
shake hands with men
like a dog and lick
the legs of women.

But like an amoeba
it makes love
in secret
only to itself.

Its food is normal
American food.
Fold it frequently;
it needs exercise.

Water it every three days
and it will repay you
with displays of affection.

Then one day when you think
you are its master
it will turn its head
as if for a kiss
and bite you gently
on the hand.

There will be no pain
but in thirty seconds
the poison will reach your heart.

Autumn

I

On the overgrown road
where nobody comes
Autumn is an old house
that has never been lived in.

The blank walls sag,
lean trembling
as if undecided which way to fall.

They have no color but grey,
the bone color.

Their dampness
is not of this century.

But the house shall not fall.
Ever.

II

Ages ago the wind broke the panes
and planted the glass
that has not yet come up
but is growing surely,
germinating in the mud.

That glass will one day bloom,
poke out through the clay
like blades,

flourish in the sun
and stand like bushes
of cheap jewelry
waiting to ambush the traveler
who has not come for centuries
and probably will never come.

The spangled bushes!
If anyone were alive
he would think they burn.

But they are cold.

Birds shall eat of them
and die.

Dirty Thoughts

Priests told me they were my enemies
so when I was young I rebuffed them,
excluded them from my parties,
and cut them cold in the street.

If they wept,
they wept in private.

Their quiet patience
outlasted my friends.
Their simplicity
put my lovers to shame.

Through the years
I have grown
accustomed to them.

They are here now.

If you are very quiet
you can hear them
in the next room
singing.

Perspective

I love people
she said
from a distance.

Everything in perspective.

Look over there toward the horizon.

No, no. More to your left.
Right where I'm pointing.

See it now,
that black dot in the landscape?

That's
my love.

Morning Moon

The barbarians in the hills
are sharpening their weapons.

All night the ghosts of Indians
have been reeling through darkness

drinking their courage,
their faces smeared with grief.

The drum of the blood
takes up its message.

The full moon hangs low
over Madison, Wisconsin,

like a chip from a statue
of an ancient civilization.

Yellow as from age.
Red as from fire.

Fallen Tree Elegy

I say this tree is much like a man
asleep, his arms cushioning his head

like branches, or a man dead, who has
renounced all but his final position.

No more shall rise these limbs in pride
to battle with the raging wind.

No more the roots like fingers
stretch themselves for water.

Shorn at root he was, betrayed by iron,
bled white to other purposes than elegance.

I say this tree is like a man
whose fruit shall never bloom.

Hard and final it fell from the sky,
smashing the arms outstretched in protest.

The crash of its death
annihilates all thunder.

Summer Night

Along the road
the shadows of dogs
wait for the moon.

Mailboxes hold out
their empty hands.
Crickets sing
the hymn to silence.

The lonely, the abandoned
wrap themselves in ditches
and sleep.

Beyond the hill
the soft voice
of the mother of violence
is calling her children
home.

Grief

When I was introduced to Grief
I was prepared for anything
but the joy-buzzer in his hand.

They laughed.

He slapped my back and slid
the chair out from under me,
and there I was on my bottom
right in the middle of the room.

What does it mean? I asked.

Nothing, he whispered.
Then the tears came.
Now you know. Nothing.

Inscription on an Altar of the Dead

"The lord is God of the living only;
the dead have another God."
—THE WANDERINGS OF CAIN

What would you do here, you seekers of signs,
burn incense to him of no name,
offer the fruits of the field,
the fat calves of your flocks?

Behold, no place is sacred to him,
nor none unfit for the terrible
celebration of his ritual.

Patience alone shall lead you
on the one-way road to his dominion
which you shall not travel at present
but waits insistently your footstep.

And who shall intercede for you before him?
High he is, and unappeasable as mountains.

None have claimed his graces
though much was accomplished
in the name of his intercession.

The fairest virgin lay bare upon the rock
and the first-born flower of your love
bowed to the knife, but all, all was vain.

You bearers of grain, givers of cattle,
take thought of your senseless gifts;
and you who reluctantly lead your children
to the blood-covered stone, consider:
neither knowledge, virtue, nor death
prevails to certainty. Go home.
Cover your heads and weep.
Your sacrifice is not acceptable.

GAIL DUSENBERY

I carried with me poems

I carried with me poems, poems which spewed out of
   everything; I saw poems hanging from the clotheslines,
   hanging from the streetlamps: I saw poems glowing in
   the bushes, pushing out of the earth as tulips do;
I felt poems breathe in the dark March night like ghosts
   which squared and wheeled through the air;
I felt poems brushing the tops of chimneys, brushing by in
   the dark; I felt poems being born in the city, Venuses
   breaking through a shattered sea of mirrors;
   I felt all the poets of the city straining,
   isolated poets, knowing none of the others, straining;
I felt that some gazed into the March night, looking, and
   finding;
and others were running down the steep streets, seeking, and
   seeking to embrace;
and others stood in empty bookstores turning over pages
   of fellow poets whom they loved but didn't know;
and some pondered over coffee growing cold, in harshly lit
   cafeterias, and gazed at the reflections of the eaters in the
   wall-to-wall mirrors;
some dwelt on what it was to grow old;
some dwelled on love;
some had gone out of time;
some, going out of time, looked back into time, and started;

I felt all of these lives and existences, all with poems at
   their center;
I knew none of these poets;
but I felt these intimations augured well, for me, and for
   poetry;
and my steps grew big, giant steps, I bounded down Parker
   Street,
a tall, taciturn, fast-walking poets' accomplice.

The Backyard on Fulton Street

                    Plums in the sun —
deep warmth, bursting darkness; ripeness;
sun in the air like a honeycomb, delicate sun-sifted
    hexagonal changes; attenuated hexahedrons,
            shifting toward the warmth,
fluttering hexahedron shapes of love, in the warm drafts –
                    vast seas of grass waving on the
                                    turf;
            and the plum tree's roots sinking through the
                                    crust,
        fluttering nerve-tip roots; grass nerves fluttering in
                                    the sun;
                bee-wings, butterflies and
                    plums, more than the visible —
        a high thin voice of love, clear pure
            gold wires humming.

New Year's

I've been a bird of night,
but this once, watching day break,
I am ashamed of my plumage,
my honors, my feathers.
It's the damp
calm. waiting. which breaks
my heart: the quiet park, the bridge,
the dark harbor, the
trees, damp in the wind,
no birds of prey, nothing
rich or silver or with trappings,
but all this white. gathering. stillness,
wet. wind wet, and closing toward
rest and
white. white. opening
everywhere.

Midnight on March 27th

Midnight on March 27th
a car door slams; there are voices on the sidewalk;
my desk is covered with papers:
the kitchen faucet drips in the sink;
all the undone dishes wait for me —
is it clear outside, is it cold;
am I forcing myself?

Letter to Duncan

Noise, business, and failures,
out of the Kazbek night hunting for records,
black, Venus hanging above the Panhandle,
in Paris they wear striped shirts,
here the man drops pills,
carries a gun,

Don't put me out, baby,
my voice cried out in my dream,
sitting on the green steps making love,

I want to tell you, teacher, with the tambourine beating,
and my head, and five Empirin,
and a statistical typing job for tomorrow,
how it is,
noise, business, typing and failures,
searching for the nearly invisible gleam of Venus,
eating white bread and butter, drinking, bad for the liver,
face working strangely, crooked smile, twisted head,
that it is hard and I can't make it,
forward, this way, any longer,

out of those green days, the halls lined with seashell,
mother-of-pearl faces bending down toward me, the sea
                                        sounds,

the chambers,
the reverberating OM of a long neighing call and farewell,

shifted into a mindless autumn with the dry rattle of
                                        tambourines,
mannequins in the hall with my clothes on,
cracked faces where the two sides of the smile don't meet,
— the world, the scene, far-out and gone, with no retainers.

The Guitar

Sing in my love's ear tonight
while he sleeps,
sing to him that mama darklove
waits with snake-kisses
beneath the pines,
waits to embrace him and draw him down
into the treetrunk
netherworld
of roaring stoves and salt kisses
and warm faded quilts,
bruise his ear, poem, with your love for him,
make an opening in his dream,
so she can come to him.

The Shadow

This is a civilization at war, and
    I am at sea in my mind, high,

at war with myself, or
resting, nor caring,

for war, content to let it
be headlines.

I have never seen suffering, Guernica,
Jews, the black dream, but now

rumblings.   Omens of death.   In the
streetstalls, the titles,
revolution impending,
death, the high
frenzy the tone
takes and no
one to
brake it.

Saturday Night

Curry odors, mustard in the kitchen,
sweet watermelons in the air; a stealthy drift of LOVE
from room to room;

the jeweled smiles twinkling in the air;
the beadgame being played everywhere.

The Opening Session of Congress Rock and Roll

Wide across the plains . . burning grass; the buffalo of
Omaha;

snow-capped peaks, the rank shoulders, dry rock,
glistening, scrub pines, dirt, the
massive boulders glinting in
the sun   sulphur jetting
out of the earth,

Old Faithful, of Liberty, native sons on the earth, hoes, and
cards,
the Pinole Inn, hard drinks, roadhouses, cars in
Montana,

freedom sunburn sidewhiskers an old man with
a gold nugget in his
tooth old hands
old wood the
metal pan
for
washing gold
out of the earth; Indians
in ragged clothes, baskets of pine
bark and wampum from a longhouse in the east
shells
on lake Michigan, Ouisconsin, Minneapolis; strong-man,
he-man, hey,
skinny Charles Atlas; posing
brawn manifest, destiny
of will or buffalo
and plains;
wild men, their teeth
flashing in their mustaches,
two Colts hanging from their belts, and
a banjo, in the cave, an old
woman with a pail of water,
soup, or laundry, for
the revolutionary
Instant-Men
in her

bound by ages, rock, stalactite,
   crystal secret hidden in her
      den, mother, Bear-Mother,
         berries for her young,
pawing honey hives in sun-light stones, mountains,
   down the rocks, the rolling acres,
      the boulders in the canyon,
        free, stands erect,
            American man.

TV and IBM, ICBM, ACLU, AACP, and CIO,
   signals flashing in a storm
      drenched union, nation,
         plains, mountains,
            eastern watershed, the lakes,
               huge emptying basins
               barges; teenage girls with pony tails
and white wool socks, and saddle shoes,
   camped in the woods, girl scouts,
      the Indian call; bone
        whistle; blood beating
          to the tomtoms in
          the earth
          they stand
          on:
          Girl Scouts
        of the world, turn on,
grow pot, string beads, throw tents
   open to your tramping kin,
      kissing cousins,
                 weaving grass, the angels' hair,
                baskets, games with high-
                faluting titles:
                secret initials,
              the hood of closeness,
            bonds in blood, same stock, same

family tree, poplar or
cottonwood waving on
the Iowa prairie, meadow-larks;
the linden in New York; in Forest Hills the
sycamores, the tennis courts, the knowing youth
with scholarships to the great institution,
Government, until the President is
twelve years old, a native son,
a genius, Savio, Bob Dylan,
giving the beat to a
Congress that is
making
peace,
in
Latin
church American language
hip to the restive shadows of the
old, the ghosts, laid free to the wind the thread
across the spindle in its own
particular pattern, spin-
ning discs of plastic
sound or round or
square TV tubes,
the opening
session
of
congress
rock-and-roll.

DAVE ETTER

Evangelist

Take my right hand
yes my right hand
plant it as seed
then let rain fall
and let sun fall
celebrate this day
run the red dogs
through the streets
of your sullen towns
through the farms
wasting away with
corn corn corn
and nervous with
the caw-caw of crows

A new day comes
is coming has come
beans beans beans
we want no beans
blow some brassy
money marches
arise you hicks
husks of Lincoln
take my right hand
plant it as seed
then stand you back
and watch me work
for Jesus Christ
and Illinois

The Red Nude

When I haven't any blue, I use red.
—PABLO PICASSO

Red candles. Smoky red lights.

Sipping a glass of claret,
the nude girl moves to the window.

The sun sets. Scarlet poppies. Bloodroot.

Pomegranates along a brick wall:
the flushed faces of old gardeners.

Under the cold strawberry stars,
crimson eyes of dying animals.

A dream of cherries and cardinals.

The ruby moon slips between
bare thighs of garnet and rosewood.

Red candles. Smoky red lights.

St. Dexter's Fire

Oranges and lemons whirl around
in a jukebox of insane guitars.

A scowling Cherokee beats a tom-tom.

Bearded, pale-lipped, and quiet,
they call me "St. Dexter."

But I have heard "Communist" and "queer" too.

I sit on this corner barstool every night,
drinking beer, gin, and shots of Scotch.

I have spent a lifetime doing nothing at all.

Once in a sunfield of silver bells
I was stoned by a pack of girls.

Now I walk through a door marked KINGS.

Behind the plugged toilet bowl
I write JESUS HAS CRAPPED OUT.

The jukebox martyrs a saxophone.

I drop a match in the used towels
and marry myself to an alley of eyes.

Red guitars. Flames. St. Dexter's fire.

Country Graveyard

Cows with eyes of buttered moons
doze along the barbed wire.

Weeds grow to impossible heights.

I call out my family names
across the camp sites of stones:
Etter, Wakefield, McFee, Goodenow.

Cedar trees shake fat crows
from their ragged beards.

In the farmhouse back from the road
shades are drawn against noon sun
and grace is said before the meat.

I stand among these gravestones
where a wet-nosed wind coughs
gray dust on my pinching shoes.

The rusty bells of the brick church.

Goodenow, McFee, Wakefield, Etter.

Firewood Hill

Toads are tamping down cakes of moss
where Potter's Lake pocks the yellow grass.

On the far slopes of Firewood Hill
there is a nude in every tree.

We are escaping from a madman's house.

We are herons with blazing wings.

We are flying to the breasted trees,
chased by a hunchback with banker's eyes.

Our heaving bodies are wild with love.

The old locks of many heavy doors
are clicking, clicking in our ears.

We are grass and leaves and firewood now.

Prairie Summer

(*For Carl Sandburg*)

1

Hollyhocks are blooming in schoolyards
of towns along the Soo Line.

In chicory lots Chevrolets rust
under the Clabber Girl signs.

In Winneshiek County, Iowa,
near where Hamlin Garland once lived,
a whole Norwegian family
is out planting apple trees.

2

Our village of rambler roses
contains cats in trellised shade,
children asleep on islands of moss,
and quiet men who smoke pipes and sit
on stone benches at the courthouse.

3

Heart-shaped leaves fall in the pitcher
of lemonade: 3¢ a glass, 3¢ a glass.

4

Dripping with a sticky green sweat,
my brother, who would be farmer,
walks the highway to Plato Center.

The endless cornfields swell above him.
Heat waves jump up from the concrete.

To breathe deeply is to half drown.

5

The barber's son brings me a gift:
13 butterflies in a cellophane bag.

The grass shudders in the lawnmower.

A bluejay screams in the jaws of the sky.

6

Under the oak tree by the back fence
my beautiful blonde sister
is writing a poem about Altgeld.

Dinner pails are in it. And picks and shovels.
Slow footsteps on broken stairs are in it.
And angry men with Polish names.
Darrow is in it. And Debs and Sandburg.

Next week she will read it aloud
to the Women's Club and the DAR.

7

Below a bluff of yellow tombstones
two houseboats gather old shadows
and the waves of a speedboat.

Time for bare feet, beer, and box scores.

8

What do sunflowers talk about after dusk
when the wind goes down and the moon comes up?

9

I love to sit here on the screened porch
and go over the names of prairie towns:
Morning Sun, Carbon Cliff, What Cheer;
and the Indian names of rivers:
Wapsipinicon, Kishwaukee, Pecatonica.

10

After the band concert in the firefly park
katydids sing above a circus of weeds—
weeds that are hiding a whiskey bottle,
a new baseball, and a book of magic.

11

Midnight: rain beats on the clapboards,
soaks the grass, cleans the walks.

Wonderful, the smell of tomato vines.

Far off, the lusty wail of diesel horns:
beef to Chicago, tractors to Omaha.

12

Tomorrow, bumbling among bees,
I will be fisherman,
seeker of lost railroads,
and ambassador to all the forgotten
kingdoms of Chautauquas and streetcars.

The Words

I carry boulders across the day
From the field to the ridge,
& my back grows tired.
A few, stubborn, in a field drawn
To old blood by the evening sun
& trembling muscles, remain.
These chafe my hands,
Pull away into the black soil.
I take a drop of sweat
Onto my thumb,
Watch the wind furrow its surface,
Dream of a morning
When my furrows will shape this field,
When these rocks will form my house.
Alone, with heavy arms,
I listen thru the night to older farms.

305 Honda

for Gary Snyder

Leaving a forest of bikes,
Leaving the university, headed for San Francisco.
　　[After watching the wistful look
　　　at a different set of handlebars, a wider grip,
　　　a deeper control.]
Leaning into the curve, sliding along the arm
of inertia,
settling into the traffic, edging around it,
headed for San Francisco.

Move forward, hold onto me, not the bike.
Find the center
of gravity,　　　　　　　　the Buddhist

Oneness & uniqueness.
Leaning against the arm of the curve.
Two poets   personal perceptions
one rider, multi-armed, -legged.
Point of intimacy:
from the first tools,   crafts,
metals & men laboring, hot, sweat
wetted, laboring with flesh & minds.
Fires & dreams, fires & gradually the machines.
The long sight.
The whole technology, a series
of carefully timed openings, man with his fire
manipulating the frozen rhythms
of road surfaces,
the intricate network of wind-rivers, the falls,
lurches,   sudden eddies.
A line of intended movement.
Be loose & heavy
against the movement's changes.
The changes—
we throw our movements out,   read them
& prophesy.

Along a bay shore highway,
wind falling loose, snapping tight with a whipped
crack at my ear, past drift-wood sculptures
on mud-flats —a sailing ship, a
locomotive, a huge & angry Indian—
movie sets, but with a looser texture, allowing
the different movements of sea & sky to show thru.
Past —leaning to the curve, headed for the tollgate
& the rise of the bridge.

A quarter given, a brief touch of a stranger's
hand, shoulders moving in front of me
& the bike jumping up over the bay, drawing
the winds into the center—

the bay like any sea, the lands rushing into the
center,
the carefully timed movements of man & his fire.

The other poet calling
back
over his shoulder,
the voice cut loose, drawn thin,
wavering,   snapping past my ear.
Gone.   Missed.
A strange wind-eel, wavering, curious,   vanished.
The silent wind-eels crawling like ropes
over my forehead, thru my hair, down my neck.
Vanishing.
Wind-eels edging around my glasses, pulling
at them.   Testing my vision.
Crawling into my eye-sockets, changing the shape
of things seen—
the shape-changers, the wind-flowing
& sounds of rice-paddy girls
& distances.

The bridge supports reach up,
drop back, & the wind rushes down, pushes at us,
keeps up its peculiar chants & animal cries, comes
out of the void & sings of the invisible planets,
suns, distances; & the changed landscape sits
in its new perspectives, indifferent
to the wind-rivers, silver & muted violets, the poems

at the edges of the bay
large shapes at the edges of the bay, chiseled
out of light
            the rough sketches, reaching out of
sight, nature's poems   & the clumsy rectangles
& silent windows of man's,

the edges of the grounds carefully surveyed, the hours
of construction computed, paid for.

The cathedral chants of the wind; we lean to the curve,
falling into the shadow
of the city. Our sound larger, now, than the wind-rivers'.
Words coming back,
& a heaviness, & the old geometries carrying us over
subdued hills;
falling into the shadow & headed
for a vodka martini.

Shaman Song 2

on taking a coal from the fire
in naked fingers

The word
is in the hand.
Under the moon
in the hand.
At the head of the valley
in the hand.
It glows in the hand.
Here!
Look here
in the hand.
Look at the word
in the hand.
It glows.
A great translucence
in the hand.
Go thru the translucence
in the hand.
Into the world
in the hand.

The coals glow
in my fire.
Are words
for the hand.

Shaman Song 10

each man's lust is a cult

The rains are warm.
Our valleys and plains are almost green
    —under blades of grass so slight
    a blade is seen only by a keen eye
from the height of a walking man.

The strong women who have borne sons are restless.
The ripe girls who have come thru the winter
    watch the sun walk across the day.
Their eyes gentle as the wind, tender as the new grass.

The shaman's tent is prepared for fire and dances.
The ripe girls who have come thru the winter
    watch the sun go away across the day.
The men look at the girls' throats and breasts in wonder.

        Night lands, breathes
its strange winds around our closed tents, and fires
breathe their forms onto the circling hides.

    Women must be torn from girls in a cruel stench
of dance filld flesh and full thighs.

    On stretcht hides of the shaman's tent
woman Gods mimic the first wild dances
        —thundercloud dancers in a sacrament.

Stolen tusk of a grandfather buffalo.
Unfalling carvd phallus of our tribe.
My corded arm is painted to the elbow
in the red rains of our Spring.

The sudden women shine at the river, trickt
from winter with a dance's thundercloud rise.

The rains are warm, our valleys and plains green.

Shaman Song 12

We have made hawks
that fly
where no hawks have flown.

We have made hard sky
and look out at the rain.

We have made warm hides
from no animal yet slain.

We have made horses
that stride
as no horses ever known.

> *But, we are weak.*
> *On our wounded plains, we are alone.*

We have forgotten
the shape and cry of our bellies.

We have forgotten
the dances of our own faces,
the songs of our own voices.

We have forgotten
the chants of the souls
in our running feet.

> *Now, we remember.*
> *In our weeping tents, we are alone.*

3 Meditations

i

"Eskimos have 17 words for snow...."

       monks ask

ancient masters
      eyes reflect
         quick rivers
      teeth are sharp
      knotted hands
        hold sticks

where is buddha

long fingers

        peach pits
bent trees
cattle droppings
striking with sticks

there is buddha

my time came to ask
the question came

where am i

      peach pits
  bent trees
  cattle droppings
  striking with sticks

call back
what you have sent out

buddha

ii

"If you try to see me through my form,
or if you try to hear me through my
voice, you will never reach me and will
remain forever a stranger to my teaching"
—GAUTAMA SIDDHARTHA

a stone
sits in the stream
a sound of passing

iii

"I had a dream last night
I don't understand my dream
But i know everything is all right, now"
—AN INMATE: SAN QUENTIN 1958

i am back

where do you think
you have been

here

Whore

i

she undressed slowly
with a sense
of the moon among clouds
stretched
to take up the belly's
beginning slack
snapped out the saffron bulb
to silhouette herself
beside the moon
she copied

ii

she washed off
her cunt
with the slow care
of a craftsman
for his tools
fingering the lips
figuring the years

she rung out
her wash rag, twisting
worn threads
dry

DAN GEORGAKAS

Harvest Song
(*after Papagoan ritual song of corn musicians*)

hi hiana hu
our songs commence.
grow strong.
he hi he
the tongues of songs
are rainbows.
hi hiana hu
are you asking?
.or do you bring?
he hi he
here upon black fields
comes forth Corn.
our happy children take it.
play!
he hi he
here upon our mother
comes forth Squash.
our singing women take it.
kiss!

Lament

(*after a death song by the Fox Indians*)
It is we, it is we.

The Eagle taketh the spirit of the Vulture.
It is we, it is we.
The Eagle taketh the spirit of the Vulture.
It is we, it is we.

All the nations are weeping, weeping
Because the Eagle is dying, dying
Because the Eagle is dying, dying
All the nations are weeping, weeping

The sun, too, shall weep.
The sun
At this end of us;
The sun, too, shall weep.

As soon as he learned

As soon as he learned
the Cubans had put a nigger
at the head of their army
he knew, for sure, they were
a bunch of goddam reds

                the angry general
                explained that
                his guerilla force
                would have succeeded
                if the goddam people
                hadn't intervened

Consider these Greek widows of America

Consider these Greek widows of America
completing black clad lives
in the rented rooms of the old neighborhood
or dreaming alone in their aging homes
now that children sleep in the wedlock
so eagerly sought for them
but which strangely had no place
for those rough skinned peasant girls
who once were matched to older men
and now endure November graveside days
sipping the last of the homemade wine.

The Scene Pope John Wouldn't Let Fellini Film

Tape   collage   sound   bursts
conducted by Karl Heinz Weissner
in stolid old Heidelberg
where the student prince drowned
in the gigantic wein stube
only a German would be gross
enough to perpetuate with dwarfs
locked arm in dunklewald singing
because *ja-ja* they are always wanting
to liberate their subliminal demons
and if just once they'd shape their genius,
refine that fantastic myth capacity
we would hear the glorious 9th pouring
from every beer hall until that exalting
silence . . . and the piping bum-ta-ta
of a three-piece Bavarian tanz band
with all the clowns, burghers, lovers
fathers of the ecumenical council
parading round & round the space ship
up the iron scaffold like a stupendous
circus Noah act of two by holy two
until safely locked in the capsule—
they blast off for the stars!

The acrobat from Xanadu disdained all nets.

The acrobat from Xanadu disdained all nets.
And when we saw him performing the central
twirl of his triple forward roll thru space
we knew his purity went beyond mere pride,
that certain flights require total risk.

Hiroshima Crewman

Somewhere in California
his body humbled by a hair shirt,
a vow of silence on his lips,
a Hiroshima crewman tries to find a life.
If he should ever choose to break his peace,
he might speak of death by fire
no Nazi ordered; he might tell how
war produces many brands of
Auschwitz soap and Dachau lampshade.

Empire City

The Bowery bum
expresses the permanent state of your personality
which arrogantly assumes
there must be losers
who will drown in wine
that certain neighborhoods must exist
glass littered & garbage heaped
because your Lincoln Center
is carbon of Mussolini's EUR
just as the Pan Am mound of glass
is talisman
for your vampire fang of parks
unfit for night
beneath skies reddened by sulphuric dioxide
that chokes Our Lady of the Harbor
so better girdled now
than iron gated apartment windows
that cannot withstand desperate junkie robbers
because if Paris is a whore
then New York is a transvestite
more glamorous than any genuine female
yet fashioned of illusions

that succeed until the moment of ultimate
sexual truth
revealing at last
a disfunctioning defected life force
more disturbed than
the twisted psyche of the most avid consumer
of Times Square sado-maso pornography
to say nothing of the sex filled-love starved
star fucking muddle class dropouts
who Mardi Gras in the Village
or take the drug voyage
now that blacks have sealed off Harlem
from their manias
with only your "new thing" jazz
to screech some truth
which is more reflection than comment
as facile poetry carps about * LOVE *
but stands mute before
the degradation of our *demos*
needing rat powder
to survive at the worst extremes
roach sprays   &   exterminator juices
everywhere
save those canopied residences of privilege
doormanned up front
as the contradictions intensify
making of violence a new norm
but your army of 27,000 cops
is not paid to protect victims
and their brute force cannot indefinitely
occupy any city
even tho now too often we die by our own hand
struggle sadly to be strong at broken places
attempt mystic escape guilts from ancient images
as some few new men break through
that one day your fabled canyons may rot
with the gates of Babylon

for there is not power enough
among your mad computer technobrats
to heal
the deranged who speak to themselves
on your Brooklyn Bridges
the knocked out sleepers in your Bronx Zoos
the crazed commuters scurrying to Long Island greeneries
those ugly faces
so plentiful on your finest Fifths of Avenues
because all the tongues & talents & visions
of your heroic immigrants
have not been strength enough to resist
the automat-ed smelting pot of dreams gone bad
so that however much your museums seek apotheosis
of capitalist realism via ersatz dada fads
and your fake historians plunge
time capsules of Empire glories
in vaults constructed to withstand
the nuclear holocaust whose brink you worship
neither they
nor your reformist mayors
nor your Malcolm executioneers
can defuse the time bombs
your unconscious hands have set
which even now commence to detonate
with the racial nightmare you have spawned
part of your cannibalistic rites
but also prelude to the new world in the making
whose humanity will no longer tolerate
the metropolitan sewers created by your
vaunted walled streets and Madhatten towers.

JOHN GILL

from Chicago

I

Chicago
the backyard
where all things start
exposed iris bulbs cluster and rot in clinker soil
stones, bones, bottles and dog poop
a catalpa tree with sickle thin cigars
we even lit them up and puffed a few
pretending to be someone like adults
there were trees of heaven along the fence
straggly and poor jesus trees they grew anywhere
and one huge shadowing dry elm
that brooded so high it didn't count
until fall when I had to rake leaves.
with smells of molding things and centipedes, beetles,
hundreds of pissy-looking weeds, some rachitic grass
barely hanging on, and a lilac whose blue
so washed out it had to be imagined
blooming, when it did, next to the garbage pail.

once this land was Lake Michigan floor
still sandy, still determined to be itself
a pledged sour rind of earth not to breed
and my earliest life dumped here
a good son of a good son of a good son
who made it from the old homestead farm
and bought this planted victorian house and yard
to hang up his golden plaque: his Doctor's sign
in staid triumph by the door. I've often tried
to conjure up the past that belongs to me but it fails—
two scotch-irish immigrant brothers, one Catesby
with many children in Havana, Ill. while my ghostly fathers
run to Indians camping on this shore
fishing, digging clams, their daily hymns of work and joy

gone, not even rubbled artifacts choked in the soil
but a child-hood honed on bare backyard alkali and weeds.

II

camping out all night in the yard
on the dark furtive ground
wrapped in home blankets to keep us warm
appalled and thrilled at our daring
we took flashlights to warn off robbers and murderers
and food to sustain our lives
(the back door unlocked in case we really got scared)
and sallied out armfuls and armfuls
the lights winking off in the house
our talk dwindled   first quaking at all noise
then less and less trembling as the moon rode free
and night bloomed dreaming its innocence
turned   my friend told me what he'd learned
from another boy—look, it gets big you stroke mine
I'll stroke yours
such palm shock such a depth spinning buzz
seized and sent floating by heels
hot hands taking turns: wonderment   disbelief
that such sensations were invented
it was this then that all parents hid!
flesh-dyed wrong but true guttural song
a winding tenuous stony terrible delicious thread
thieves and murderers stamping their way out of the ground
the moon fluttering in calm disbelief over our exposed bodies
drifting from our seed bed   ripped open   dreaming.

Frances

the body is a threshold   not a waterfall
it has to be led by the hand
won't somebody please understand what I'm saying!

the body is not a hand covering the place of shame
it's a waterfall that sends up dazzling spray
it tremors as it slides nearer the threshold
it is stronger than anyone's gaping command
I am so ashamed   heavy as a suitcase
as I step over my packed and tinselled body
won't somebody . . . there is a giant hand
it beckons me to my eternal shame
it doesn't lead   its fingers cover me
please please somebody   I'm afraid
the body is a threshold   not a waterfall
it has to be led by the hand.

"Today Well, Tomorrow Cold in the Mouth."

(old Finnish proverb)

Today, a fellow in the mirror,
a vagabond of sorts
holding the lightest reins
on himself. Today is not clear
or sharp, only a false
door that opens on hinges
either way, and either way
means freedom of choice,
theoretically at least.
Today we don't pay,
we don't hear our own voice
and time is still blest.

Tomorrow the weasel strikes
and what we've refused of pain
comes marching in
like a brass band, high

and handsome; we are shamed
and hate the crude din.
Now we know the taste
of everything we ate:
no more light youth,
no more mirrored face
swinging a balanced fate.
Tomorrow is cold in the mouth.

in defense of marriage

today, this moment, here, you love me
the pole-vaulter's holiday is coming down
boats lining the shore drift and scatter
the secular world pulls its collar
and ducks before the cold blast from the north
while in spain castanets growl and rattle
and the sun meals flesh for all it's worth.

Conjured

the shore is always a shelf
    and at night
the sands have a burnt calm
    about them.
sandpipers scoot before the waves
that spread out, foam hissing.
my God, you were lovely in that
    perpetual damp
your naked body set against
    a low hill!
the driveling push of the waves stopped
when you slipped your clothes
    and stood there

compounded of wet and dark and a
     rubbed light; risen shamelessly
as if I'd conjured you up,
heart-crying, afraid that you would burst
or waver ever so slightly
     before my eyes.

some friends

they bring with them their burden
their burden of life & living through
self   the burden of self
hung up on meat hooks on a warm day.
they can take themselves   take
anything that proves they're hung up
they can talk enough   talk around enough
so the self still blooms   still on top
even hooked on top   so what!
screws downward   maybe a lot   to compensate
but still up   hung   a burden
to carry a self it's a lot
to carry any kind of weather   especially
this self this hot this burden this day.

scène à faire

the seeds of perversion,
the original I'm afraid
that last through centuries.
the void bellowing in his ear
who threw himself wild
and desperate on her
with sudden brutality.

or he fondles her body
unable to say that now,
"helplessness and loathing
both live within me.
let me go! let me go!"
he sinks into the void
as one might smile in Hell.

or other seeds, blighted,
that yet never fail:
the peeping-tom breathing
heavily near the window,
or dreamily abuse himself
or only want young boys
or love to dress like girls.

ghosts as quick as these
gather close to him
and with his hunchback mind
he labors endlessly
to produce a single flower.
it will scud forth one day
riding the pillars of the sea.

poem

what of radishes lettuce peas
lifting out of the hard ground!
and if you could hear the strain of labor
or even imagine the unimaginable pressure
on the bent backs of the bean!
all night soaking in sweat of dew
on the mother-bedded exhaling acres
stars pricking the future above them
while worms chew and grubs curl inward
roots spreading in stony underkeep.

and then the sun diffusing a bluish light
then wave on wave mounts and shoots
vociferous to their patient sheds of green
a blinding hallelujah of fire
and yes yes yes to possibility.

the other garden

the ram in the sacred tree
mounts up happily
his lapis lazuli eyes
squint in paradise
his tail quivering

his body thin hammered gold
a face centuries old
jew-bearded, satisfied

the simple flower of the tree
bright with emerald leaves
droops aside

his horny feet knocking
he plows his chosen bride

Evoë! Evoë!
the garden (again) is sanctified.

JOHN HAINES

The Dance

For George Hitchcock

The red armchair is empty.
The man who sat there
is turning in the room,
holding in his hands
a painted jungle.

The faces of his audience,
at first like flowers
pale from lack of sunlight,
begin to darken and put on
the look of watchers
in a clearing.

No sound but a furtive
scratching, and the slow steps
turning against smoke
and silence, as the dance
gathers everything
into a haunted forest...

From the bark of those trees
sprout flowers
like drops of blood,
and birds' heads
of a threatening blue.

Moons

There are moons like continents,
diminishing to a white stone
softly smoking
in a fog-bound ocean.

Equinoctial moons,
immense rainbarrels spilling
their yellow water.

Moons like eyes turned inward,
hard and bulging
on the blue cheek of eternity.

And moons half-broken,
eaten by eagle shadows...

But the moon of the poet
is soiled and scratched, its seas
are flowing with dust.

And other moons are rising,
swollen like boils —

in their bloodshot depths
the warfare of planets
silently drips and festers.

"It Must All Be Done Over..."

Everywhere I look the houses are coming down,
the yards are deserted,
people have taken to tents and caravans,
like restless cattle breaking stride,
going off with their carts
under a rumbling cloud.

I am sometimes moved by a persistent
trembling of the landscape.
I have begun to believe those rumors
of the world's wheat being eaten
by metallic grasshoppers,

and columns of brutal strangers
advancing on the soul of Asia.
A gross and sickening shadow covers the State;
no one in power commands a listener.

In the days to come
I hope I shall be able to leave
without too much baggage
or bitterness. I must make my life
into an endless camp,
learn to build with air, water, and smoke...

The Cauliflower

I want to be a cauliflower,
all brain and ears,
meditating on the origin of gardens
and the divinity of Him
who carefully binds my leaves.

With my blind roots touched
by the songs of the worms,
and my rough throat throbbing
with strange, vegetable sounds,
perhaps I'd feel the parting stroke
of a butterfly's wing...

Not like those cousins the cabbages,
whose heads, tightly folded,
see and hear nothing of this world,
dreaming only on the yellow
and green magnificence
that is hardening within them.

Larkspur

The blue giant is passing,
king of this field.

His trumpets blow pure cobalt,
he brings with him
audiences of the deepest indigo.

By his command
the sky-stained meadows overflow,
and bridges of azure
stretch far into evening...

where the king, his train halted,
stands alone in his blueness.

Paul Klee

The hot mice feeding in red,
the angry child
clutching a blue watermelon —
these are the sun and moon.

The Tunisian patch,
where beneath some crooked
black sticks
a woman's face is burning.

There are also disasters at sea,
compasses gone wrong —

only because of a submarine
laughter
no one is drowning.

The Stone Harp

A road deepening in the north,
strung with steel,
resonant in the winter evening,
as though the earth were a harp
soon to be struck.

Or as if a spade
rang in a rock chamber —

in the subterranean light,
glittering with mica,
a figure like a tree turning to stone
stands on its charred roots
and tries to sing.

Now there is all this blood
flowing into the west,
ragged holes at the waterline of the sun —
that ship is sinking.

And the only poet is the wind,
a drifter
who walked in from the coast
with empty pockets.

He stands on the road at evening,
making a sound like a stone harp
strummed
by a handful of leaves.

The Color

It was simply a dark,
laboring mass.
Now and then it gave off

some half-stifled
animal noises.

A group of idle people
were watching.
Curious, they drew close,
and someone prodded
the mass with a stick.

Because it was hungry,
it reached out a brown,
tentative finger;
a mouth,
suddenly appearing
in its sweating flesh,
opened and closed.

The people were frightened —
a woman screamed.

They all hurriedly withdrew
and immediately began
building walls
against this amorphous,
expanding misery of color.

The Great Society

Having been whipped through Paradise
and seen humanity
strolling like an overfed beast
set loose from its cage,
a man may long for nothing so much
as a house of snow,
a blue stone for a lamp,
and a skin to cover his head.

Red Atlantis

The sodden bumping of caisson wheels,
the muffled gun-reports
as the sun sweats in its watery canyon;
this lowering of coffins, these
submarine torches
lighting the face of a tomb...

Our nation is sinking, swept
by a tide of blood.
The government a rotten hulk
through whose jammed and rusty portholes
statesmen are staring —
they make slow and deliberate gestures
as though their arms and legs
were tangled in ropes of scarlet slime.

There's an odor, faintly of sour wine;
and a twilight wind that carries
a soaked bell's ringing
like a rumor of salvation.
Overhead, in flocks like sunset clouds,
rose-beaked swallows search
with human cries; but no poet has come
with a voice hoarse and bleeding,
no man of sea-lilacs.

There are only endless funerals,
and crowds of people stunned since birth
by a crime they have not forgotten;
their clothing stiffens,
they stand to their waists
in a red shadow that is rising —

and only the blood is real,
inflamed oxygen through which the sun
sinks like a bursting diver...

PHYLLIS HARRIS

Whatever Edens

whatever Edens I may go
Bowery has gouged me
left me for dead, my guts
lodged with a rusty nail.

whose rape was real.

stench of sweat, an open fly
Bowery glared with bloodshot moon
(I was a child, I closed my eyes)
the scar burned through.

whatever sun, shall be eclipsed

I am no virgin. whatever song
my ears may wear, the rape remains;
whatever seas, that wave
still shatters drunkward from my shore.

Mandylion

"a tick can live
for 7 years
without a host, lie low
in the high grass
hoping to hitch a ride"

Christ in the ikon over the makeshift bed
where we have been moved, from our alcove
of Mexican draping over gold embroidered spread
to make room, make respite
for our uninvited Guest

welcome each wayfarer
as Christ, each wino
hophead, Queen John's
navy, Doggie Diner God

    accept him
    saint
    or psychotic

or Dean Plagowski, flaked-out
Wobbly pamphleteer, unfolding
4 handfuls of phenobarb
intended to end his career

    pariah
    or pervert
    allow him

in this ikon, where I nailed him with a staplegun
lined with a stream of Russian madonnas & Michaels
Christ, his head, appears in the shape of a tick
2 tresses, either side, are legs, the pointed
beard-mouth, halo like a swollen belly

sucks my blood: o indecorous
parasite Christ, how much kinder
you seemed to the child, small sacrament
trapped in the chalice, throned
in the gold monstrance glass

you knew
your place then
you stayed put
under glass
could be counted on, counted

never to pee on my sheets
nor crawl inside my bed, my belly
nor lean down from your most high altar
to puke in my face, on my knees

Outside

grotesque, the line of trees, pronged
branches through the fog: the low cloud
passing, granular
& self-involved.

stare out the window. don't.
their life is theirs
this one
our own.

a closed cold room. possessions.
shelves of silent words, the anger
silting down. our life
together.

back.
come back
there isn't any
where to go.

The Source

He kept his mouth forever
at the source, catching
even in drought
the few drops
coaxed
from the ancient spring

kneeling in dry grass
liking the feel of it
sparse now, parching
he stole

without malice. In floodtime
too, in plenty
he knelt with his lips
& it poured to him

still without greed
he received it, abundance
filled
& flowed from him, over
the dry earth
he soon would be

Under Your Voice, Among Legends

I.

mama writes
"your papa's
dad is gone"

he is. they ride him from the farm
in Sunday socks
comb out his beard & bless
then let him down at last
by Grandma in the thick Nebraska sod

the tin spittoon is tossed
in trash by the cistern, orchard apples
rot, the new Ford bought
the morning I was born
ruts up in mud to the runningboard

I am not there
I dream it

; he does not care

2.

the summer I was ten
I climbed rust-ragged steps
of your granary, Grandpa

to the loft where your son
the boy my father
slept

& was met in the crusted silence
by strange smells, odor
of old dreams, corn
& rotting grain

   I remember
  how the boards cried out
  beneath me, how fear
  hooked at the root of my tongue
  & the cobweb ghosts descending

  how my heart erupted
  as the red-eyed raven rose
  monstrous
  mounting the shadows

& I was plunged sobbing
into the kerosene clasp
of my grandmother's kitchen

into the warm yeast smells of Bohemian baking
prunefilled kolaches, poppyseed rolls rising

under bleached sacks, the August apples foaming
in stone vats in the pantry

3.

that summer you shot
the black mad bull, & I felt
blood of the stuck pig, hot
dung of horses

saw small deer broken in the railbed
held dead snakes at sunset
followed green-faced pheasants
grazing near the field's edge

 under your voice, among legends
 I woke to my poems
 lonely at times, curious
 companionship with the bones

 song of the Skidi maidens
 blood spun at dawn, libation
 to the morningstar Corn Mother
 chanting the grown gold out

now twenty years have burned
your stories into glass
I drink from them by day, by night
I grapple the ancient bird

hung vast & enigmatic, haunter
of granary shadows, cold
totem of knowledge, guard
of the red-eyed past

4.

here the seasons go down
stifled
      clicker of heels in the night street
city of neon dancers, the electric
drunken blood

        & I am knotted with longing
        for the old earth-handed knowledge

for Indian-eyed watchers of seasons
storm-fearing farmers, snow
on the prairie shoulders rippling
like flexed muscles in wind

for my cornsilk Christmas dolls
necklace of dried corn
yucca smell, soapweed
the incense odor of sage

for my brothers, strongnosed
in the firelight, sunburned
with the earth smell on their ankles

my sisters bent over the piano
swaying like reapers
like weavers over the keys

for the long star-fallen nights
we sat like goatherds
tending our speech

wet mornings, wistful
repetitive
velvet afternoons among the wheat gold winter weeds

      o pioneers!

      o sweet grandfather Adam

I sit in the subways among metal faces raging
as the wars roar in on transistor tracks

I race under the world city crying
for my lost home, Nebraska, my grandfather's orchard

I plant money in the asphalt

; I lunch on bitter apples

JIM HARRISON

Night in Boston

From the roof the night's the color
of a mollusc, stained with teeth and oil—
she wants to be rid of us and go to sea.

And the soot is the odor of brine
and imperishable sausages.

Beneath me from a window I hear "Blue Hawaii."
On Pontchartrain the Rex Club
dances on a houseboat in a storm—
a sot calms the water without wetting a foot.

I'd walk to Iceland, saluting trawlers.
I won't sell the rights to this miracle.

It was hot in Indiana.
The lovers sat on a porch swing, laughing;
a car passed on the gravel road,
red tail-lights bobbing over the ruts,
dust sweeping the house,
the scent of vetch from the pasture.

Out there the Baleen nuzzles his iceberg,
monuments drown in the lava of birdshit.
I scuffle the cinders but the building doesn't shudder—
they've balanced it on a rock.
The Charles floats seaward, bored with history.

Night, cutting you open
I see you're full of sour air
like any rubber ball.

War Suite

The wars: we're drawn to them
as if in fever, we sleep walk to them,
wake up in full stride of nightmare,
blood slippery, mouth deep in their gore.

. . .

Even in Gilgamesh, the darker bodies
strewn over stone battlements,
dry skin against rough stone, the sand
sifting through rock face, swollen flesh
covered with it, sand against blackening lips,
flesh covered with it, the bodies
bloating in the heat, then hidden,
then covered; or at an oasis, beneath
still palms, a viper floats toward water,
her soft belly flattened of its weight, tongue
flicking at water beside the faces of the dead,
their faces, chests, pressed to earth, bodies
also flattened, lax with their weight,
now surely groundlings, and the moon
swollen in the night, the sheen
of it on lax bodies and on the water.

. . .

Now in Aquitaine, this man is no less dead
for being noble, a knight with a clang
and rasp to his shield and hammer;
air thick with horses,
earth fixed under their moving feet
but bodies falling, sweat and blood
under armor, death blows, sweet knight's
blood flowing, horses screaming, horses
now riderless drinking at a brook, mouths sore
with bits, sweat drying grey on flanks,

noses dripping cool water, nibbling
grass through bits, patches of grass
with the blood still red and wet on them.

II

I sing sixty-seven wars; the war now,
the war for Rapunzel, earth cannot use
her hair, the war of drowning hair
drifting upward as it descends,
the lover holding his cock like
a switch-blade, war of
apples and pears beating against the earth,
earth tearing a hole in sky, air to hold
the light it has gathered, river bending
until its back is broken, death a black
carp to swim in our innards.

. . .

Grand wars; the final auk poised
on her ice-flow, the wolf shot
from a helicopter; that shrill god
in her choir loft among damp wine colored
crumpled robes, face against a dusty
window, staring out at a black pond
and the floor of a wood-lot
covered with ferns – if that wasp
on the pane stings her...
cancer to kill child, child to kill cancer,
nail to enter the wood, the Virgin
to flutter in the air above Rome like a pipercub,
giraffe's neck to grow after greener leaves,
bullet to enter an eye, bullet
to escape the skull, bullet to fall
to earth, eye to look for its skull,
skull to burst, belly to find its cage or ribs.

. . .

Face down in the pool, his great fatty
heart wants to keep beating; tongue pressed
to rug in a chemical hallway; on a country
road, caught by flashbulb headlights,
he wishes suddenly to be stronger than a car.

III

The elephant to couple in peace,
the porpoise to be free of the microphone;
this page to know a master, a future,
a page with the flesh melodious,
to bring her up through the page, paper shrouded,
from whatever depth she lies,
dulling her gift, bringing her to song
and not to life.

. . .

This death mask to harden before
the face escapes, life passes
down through the neck – the sculptor
turns hearing it rub against the door.

. . .

Mind to stay free of madness, of war;
war all howling and stiff necked dead,
night of mind punctuated with moans and stars,
black smoke moiling, puling mind striped as a zebra,
ass in air madly stalking her lion.

. . .

Fire to eat tar, tar to drip,
hare to beat hound
grouse to avoid shot

trout to shake fly
chest to draw breath
breath to force song,
a song to be heard,
remembered and sung.

. . .

To come to an opening in a field
without pausing, to move there in a full circle of light;
but night's out there not even behind the glass –
there's nothing to keep her out or in;
to walk backwards to her, to step
off her edge or become her edge,
to swell and roll in her darkness,
a landlocked sea moving free
dark and clear within her continent.

ROBERT HERSHON

In This Forest

In this forest, shorn of sky,
Dark with owls and distant snaps,
I am near to your hand,
Close with you in dust and glade,
Close with the thorns, the dark shapes.

Do not seek the owl in night.
His eye shines only for the hunt.
Do not swing the lantern wide.
There is light enough
And I am close.

In this forest, dry and torn,
There is path enough
And I am close.

Report to the Blue Guard

the problem: to remember
the dreams of the day
to report
to the blue guard
on the bridge

and i will forget
tonight again
and lie in the sun pits
uninterrogated
painted many colors

far below the bridge
standing on the bridge
with the blue guard
smoking
swaying

The Shoemaker's Booth

the million brown
discards of the lame

silent machines

sitting in my socks
rubbing my toes

the old man taps
and frowns
my shoe in his hand
the telling of a secret

stolen time
of semi-clad

i cannot run
i cannot run

i need not

We Are

we are secret things on the sky
changelings of the sun
trees in their bark
flowering within

we are a meadow a mountain
oaken armed and grassy eyed
the cypress in white leaf
calling with mossy mouths

we are the stream beneath the sea
the river through the wave

melting stones in moony beds
the silt that scorns the flood

we are a countryside a continent
a thousand running and running things
airy hawks and thunder blooming
tongues of leaping trout

we are pulling rain
by the hair down and down
to the sky on the ocean floor
to the flower locked in wood

The Zoo Club

In the roof
  of the Zoo Club
  lives a bear
     with yellow fur:
      a yellow bear
He eats lovely ladies
  In the cellar
     lives a purple (purple) hawk
  He eats ugly gentlemen
Under a chair (simply)
     lives an orange snake
He eats everybody else
  Membership is limited
  Lunch is long

Child at Sand

we built
a pregnant dead hermaphrodite snowman
with a bleached chablis cork penis
and shell teeth that might draw blood

lizzie put
a small white pebble on each tit
confident the earth has a nipple
(at the north pole where the mexicos live)

Midtown Poem

I have swallowed my nearest and dearest
and my stomach has grown huge

Bless me I carry a child
and its mother and all mothers

Lord such a grand gut
I've hired twelve whining boys

as porters   When we board a bus
Paul Bunyan screws the Lincoln Tunnel

One day children I will unzip
Heads and arms will tumble forth

and run like a tide down Broadway
I'll fill the sagging bag with ash

purse my fleshy lips and give
slices for nickels on the great white way

On Horror

If it is horrible to be burned alive by savage tribesmen
who dance and leap about as your wrist watch melts,
        it is horrible to be burned by a hot pot.

If it is horrible in the great gothic house when the hairy claw
comes through the velvet drape and clutches your throat,
 it is horrible when your child touches your hand as you
 sleep.
If it is horrible when the fiendish vaudevillian, in a rage
 because
you were in the fourth grade with his wife, pins you to the
 wall
with his wicked throwing knives and takes dead aim at your
 breast pocket,
 it is horrible to mince onions.
If it is horrible to be buried under an avalanche of snow and
 rocks
set off by a mad alpinist, shrieking in the thin air,
 it is horrible to drop a book on your toe.
If it is horrible to be drowned in the relentless flood as you
 were racing
to warn the FBI that bearded saboteurs were lurking near
 the dam,
 it is horrible to scrub your feet in the bath.

But if the pot boils without heat?
If the child's eyes are dark, the infant prowling?
If the book, new to your eyes, curses your name?

There is horror in all love, in the sweet apple.
The mouth cannot taste it, the hand cannot feel it.
Horror is small and warm and damp
and wears your mother's dresses.

German Eyes

german eyes are counting your teeth
quickly in the pumpernickel   too late
the baron has returned from prague
with news of your shirts

miss fry is not really a maid
she uses your perfumed soap   too late
you have been warned   i have warned you
you have been watched   i have watched you
they'll hang us all
you first

Loves of the Public Servants

the firemen are in love
o red loves brass
the policemen are in love
o blue loves wood
the gardeners are in love
o green loves steel
the judges are in love
o black loves wool
the hose the stick
the rake the gavel
naughty public servants
who do not love
the striped flesh
of the secret peddler

Paintings of Roses

paintings of roses
just roses
you taught me to see them
shades of red
the birth and death of red
celebrations of the absence
of red
the fat madness
of rose upon rose

commiseration of the leaves
not red
this is not the way to die
this is not the way
to live

How To Walk in a Crowd

never pass a nun
on the left

never walk behind
children
they hold hands

never look up
you'll trip
on the blind man's
dog

watch for people
growing apart

never be afraid
of gutters holes
cracks pale canes
sleeping cops

never stop
for greetings
it's a plot

when the sign
says DONT WALK
crawl

the woman beside
you at the curb
has fallen dead
she'll get
a ticket

After

You might climb up to heaven,
   or cycle through from hell,
      to find a toad,
a mule, a roach or two.
     Does not the dog eat meat,
   the loon eat fish, the goose shun fire?
Are there no mules of honor, toads who die
     for swamp and flag?

Or you might be dust,
    gliding over meadow dung,
  at one with kings and weevil eggs.
Will not the wren alight, the whale seek air,
    the lion rot?

WILLIAM M. HOFFMAN

Marrakech

It took two hours, then six,
to go to Marrakech—
this is my last poem to you,
my dear; my love is dying—
because I was lonely in rainy Paris.

One morning—the room was as damp as yours was when
we came back from Bryn Mawr—I called someone by your
name.

Paris is familiar from pictures. But go there. I will give you
names to look up. You will go there.

I have sent you an unsigned carbon of this poem, although
it is dedicated to you, so that your copy will have no value.

Casablanca, Detroit with palm trees, quickly passed through,
then Marrakech:

The Koutoubia, an eleventh-century mosque in gardens
of reddish crumbling brick. Excessive and exaggerated in the
clear air.

Djama'a el Fna, a market place the size of Washington
Square, with Negro dancers from the Atlas Mountains, story
tellers, snake charmers, and the smell of broiling half-decayed
meat, snails, mackerel, mint tea, donkeys, and veiled women.

The Menara Gardens, olive trees and a pool of algae and
dying fish.

Marrakech is unfamiliar, except to you. You were born in
Marrakech, where they understand the value of love.

Love is kouskous.
Love is a bed.
Love is water.
Love is shade.

Europe is expensive. It costs two trillion seven hundred
eighty-nine billion dollars. For this money you will get
        a fine collection of Rembrandts
        and antique French furniture—
        just like you saw on Third Avenue
        and in the Frick—
        towers,
        ruins,
        a whole civilization,
        service compris.
Morocco is cheaper. Perhaps you will meet someone who
can afford Morocco.

My love is dying. I cannot afford to feed it. It is disconnected, almost evicted.

I'll end with an incantation:
        By the skies of Holland,
        by Notre Dame and Saint Germain,
        by our love as it was—
        revive, revive—
        by the roses and boys of Marrakech,
        may food and money
        bring you concerned arms
        and eyes to watch you sleep.

Mustache

In the *Book of Beards and Accomplishments of Men
Crossing Oceans and Inventing Fire*,
where does his mustache figure,
scented with beer and Evelyn's translucent lipstick?

The ambition to act in accordance with the ease
of a slow fuck in the meadows of her breasts,
a kind mother breeze cooling his ass,

or of noting with magic marker on large sheets
the nova spark fires of connotative thought.

Or simply to make more of himself,
bending space to his curvature,
especially around the head.
(How cold space is without him in it.)
To fill the hallway with hair pictures.

Or, finally, to make mustache music,
will he won't he eye riffs,
puffs of corn starch, chocolate smells,
attached with nylon thread
to his young teeth.

holy light equally lights
To J.D.

holy light equally lights
within without withal
flowing from iris to object
apples! hanging or fallen
and your cheek as easily bruised
so be it
as an apple an apple

lying here in yellow leaves
eyes belying twisting aright
the descending trees
only our hands tell true
infinite objects
grass and sod
back and hair
except
ah

so be it
breathe and prove it
as sweet as myrrh
breathe air
and again except
so be it
taste apple

Screw Spring

Screw spring.
I'm the only thing not blooming.
The arrowhead plant,
so carelessly potted,
is growing godammit.
Even the jonquils,
bought for one dinner,
are not quite dead.
Under the bed
the dust is as thick
as wool on spring sheep,
which are undoubtedly
grazing where
grass is growing
at an enviable rate.

Screw spring.
My boyfriend's taken
to getting up early.
He goes out
to see plants
pushing their way
out of the ground,
and flowering,
and sits by some chartreuse tree
in the sun, breathing air
as sweet as berry wine,

watching girls pass.
Their faces are rested
from sleeping alone all winter.

Screw spring.
I wish it were winter,
when the world's
this one room.
These walls, this bed
do
not
grow.

The Cloisters

Fort Tryon Park: September

Alone in these woods
among vagaries of leaves,
pale arcades,
and plummeting berries,
we founder
and flee into dreams
of permanence.

The sun, diminished by trees
and blackening ivy,
the filtered sun, falters.
Homeless, we seek
the cobbled court,
where our laughter
rises like pigeons.

Song to the Witch of the Cloisters

To J.C.

Old lady in the herb garden,
this Sunday in the lavender,
fat lady in the crawling leaves,
white lady in the sun,
I know by moonlight,
sweet lady, what you are.

Granny, Granny, the lovers wake
and, oh, they sigh and fold.
White shades glow like stained glass;
their cigarettes burn like incense.

Mistress who rules coriander
and curbs scents without mercy,
in whose palace grows
the woven pomegranate,
help me stop that stirring,
without me willing,
their kissing, their sleeping, their soaring.

My lady of the Cloisters,
where Mary is forever weeping,
the holy baby never wakes,
and Christ lies unresurrected,
before the moon moves
and is laced gently by leaves,
make the lovers be still.

The Unicorn
To L.W.

Now, now as buds grow
and snow melts in parks—
and black before, far away,
the trees verge purple
on the Palisades—
pale boy,
make clear how you stand
in relation to tulips
and, after, languor
in the green blast of the sun.

Now, now before asphalt buckles
and this grass-starved city
grows weeds in the street,
quick boy, come to me cold—
let our swell and sweet bend
warm these woods—

                    lest
spring catch you three nights sad,
when fog obscures the bridge
and stars shimmer in the arc-lamp haze;
lest tubers and tendrils and red oak,
yellow streamers,
and the smell of mud and river
catch the unicorn
who thinks love, like vision,
proceeds from *his* eyes.

EMMETT JARRETT

Runes

I picked up six black stones on the beach today,
put them still damp in my pocket and brought them home to
    play with,
forgot them for a while, eating supper, then remembered
and took them out, dry now, to look at.
I laid them out one by one on the table under the lamp:
a large one, a flat one, one round, one square,
one with a trace of copper like a wire fence separating two
    fields,
and one with a long nose down the middle of its face,
both eyes on one side, one under the other —
an ugly little fellow but likely to inspire fear and obtain
    worship.
Dried out now, in the light, they are all pock-marked and
    gray:
the six black stones I picked up walking on the beach
this January day.

Invitation

Come out of the classroom, Katya,
Stop teasing your teacher and come get in bed with me.
I want to strip off your anxious innocence like clothes,
Undo your white-ribboned pigtailed hair
And let your black hair fall down over your angular
    shoulders and little breasts to your knees
And be your only covering.
You're not a child any more and not a woman yet.
You're going to become a woman whether you like it or
    not and it disturbs you,
I can see it when you turn suddenly around in your chair
And throw five at your sister a year older than you.
You can't stand the insult of her womanly grace, rounded
    ankles, her knowing eyes that know too much and
    nothing any more of what you know, Katya.

Bring me your untouched body
Instinctively covering yourself like Venus with childish
    immodest hands.
Bring me your hips that are not rounded out just yet,
Bring them quickly before you become just another
    fat-assed Greek woman dropping children like sweat
    on hot days.
Bring your artlessly coy, graceless, all-knowing body into
    my bed,
I will open your tight little cunt up with my tongue,
My tongue is warm and moist.
You won't feel any shame, you will never lose the fight
    that is even now being secretly withdrawn from your
    body, how and by whom you don't know.
Come to my bed and I will open you up with the same
    gentle violence your eyes have and your awkward body
    asks for.
You will be child and woman at once.
Your teasing will be true, Katya.

From *Design for the City of Man: A Vision*

Overture

The city is in imminent danger of being destroyed;
Certain sojourners rejoice at the news.

Once old men fished in the Seine,
Boys swam naked in the Hudson and graceful girls
Played in the green hills around Florence.
Fine olives grew from a single tree
On the akropolis of Athens and even before
Beautiful women played with the bulls at Knosos.

Then walls were built
That could only be burned down
On a day when the wind blew steady from the south;
The olive withered, careless hands dropped statues
And perfect poems were used to wrap garbage in.

A second chance was offered
But within thirteen years it was bartered
For commercial advantage, unrealized.

Now a catatonic rules over orderly chaos
With weapons he lacks the wit to design;
The citizens are turned out of the gates
To eat locusts and wild honey.

The city is in imminent danger of being destroyed;
Certain sojourners rejoice at the news.

Two Mad Songs

The Young Girl's Song

I gave birth to the sun,
Nursed him in a cavern
Under the warm sea.

I raised him up as my son
And brought him forth
In the morning, shining.

He grew up in an hour,
Shone on the round world,
Then came back to me.

All in a single night
I bore him, nursed him,
Reared him to brightness

And buried him,
All in the same warm sea.
I am again with child.

The Young Man's Song

I am the cock of the world:
I love my mother.

I was conceived by the moon
On a starlit night,

Rocked in her slender arms.
Then I loved her and she—

(Laughing and biting)—
Swelled up like a white balloon.

She set me down on the ground
To play with my brothers.

We tug at the moon with her tides,
Nibble at wild-goat figs.

I am the cock of the world:
I love my mother.

from "The Sojourners"

Under the flower
That blooms this morning,
Traces of snow, traces
       of snow—
Kallakhrinaki,
A calla lily,
Smooth white mouth
       with pointed tongue—

The tongue cocks upward,
Earth-colored, ochre
The wide mouth opens
          perfectly white.

from "The City"

          Set over against lust,
Pleasure:
          No red but the red of anemones,
          only the blood of Adonis
          whose flowers sprinkle the roadside.
          Bodies are softly united,
          touching is always caressing
          for love is dancing here,
                    praised and exalted.

          Set over against money,
Pleasure:
          It can never be purchased,
          priceless, can only be given.
          No bodies are broken, flesh
          and limbs are laved
          in loving and dancing
          and we are knit together,
                    praised and exalted.

          Set over against envy,
Pleasure:
          For the time is free
          and our bones are clothed
          in amorous new bodies.
          We are isomers one of another
          and all are joined
          to our delightful dancing,
                    evermore praised and exalted.

from "The City"

In Homer's time
there were a hundred cities
    in Crete,
        my island home.
Today
there are more than 1500 varieties of wildflowers,
at least one hundred of which are indigenous.
Quince, the sweet fruit, in shape of a fig,
    is native to the island,
and the cultivated olive was introduced
into the Peloponnesos by Herakles the Cretan.
And Daidalos flew with wings
of wax and feathers,
wings of wax and feathers.
    When we tire of ascending
        the mountain
we look down from the height
    and refresh ourselves
        with the delicate colors
of wildflowers,
    God's footprints,
        blood of Adonis,
hyacinth, narcissus,
    even asphodel,
        the flower of
incredible love
    with mystic crosses
        traced
in red on its petals.

Our drink is water
for it cools the throat,
living water bathes our bodies,
we know how to give our lives completely
every day.

And God shall wipe away all tears from their eyes:
and there shall be no more death, neither sorrow, nor
crying, neither shall there be anymore pain: for the
former things are passed away.

The shape of the city
is the shape of earth, its map
imagination.
Flowers and rainbows,
the glistening
beauty of fishes,
all in fresh water,
strawberries to eat
and *stafilia*, there.

'There trees for evermore bear fruit,
'And evermore do spring;
'There evermore the angels sit,
'And evermore do sing.'

Hear the voices of birds
and understand them,
converse with animals
on terms of equality,
speak to the earth
and listen attentively
to the earth's voice.
No toil, no labor
but love's
for the joy of making.
The angels?
The angels are women
and men,
with gills and fins
to swim in the sea
and wings on their shoulders
like Daidalos' wings

of wax and feathers,
     Chagall's angels
            and Rilke's
aber nicht schrecklich,
   not terrible.

The words of the poem dance across the page,
the birds in the air dance above the clouds,
the fish in the water dance among the waves,
     love's dance.
The city is set on a hill
(Phaistos my model,
     from my island home)
no poets live there
    for all men are poets:
their songs fall
    palpable
       as golden pears
from the tree
when the breeze blows over their ripeness,
    as pears from the tree
      all the year:

Morning and evening
   spring and fall
      youth and old age and

        new life

in the city I long for
where the block is both carved
   and whole,
     the vessels
in order:
    moving at random like atoms,
     isomers one of another
modelled upon God's body:

For we have built
the city without walls.

SISTER MARY NORBERT KÖRTE

To Dance in a Loving Ring

(for Hilary Ayer Fowler)

Step
and   pattern becomes
feet like drops of
purposive water
their plash deliberate tone
to accompany their each
measure

Step
and   edge becomes
sharply rounded   leading
what is the after of our
going before
not bound to arms but
mastered

Step
and   song becomes
sings itself through figure
of arms and feet
so lastly we know
with delight overtaking caught
movement

the dance of realized pattern
            on the live edge
of fitting song

'a new flower—pure and untorn.'

—MICHAEL MCCLURE

grows within me slippery
evasive as children

almost afraid
of its beauty in awe

of the colors
the perfume penetrating

with an honest blood
the veining stems

pushing its roots to reach
always to reach always to reach

I feel its now-birth
the purity of its coming

and the wholeness of it
that passion gives until

blossoming is smoother than lilies
more hypnotic than roses

deeper than wildweed kiss
the flower of

giving   giving   spiritlife
full to burstout love

'In the most lightsome darkness'
—PICO DELLA MIRANDOLA

How I would be some night-creature of God
who moves contained in his
quiet   from mulberry to privet
with little hesitation
                    the stumble alien to his feet
his swift going sure in
            circle, pace, and halt
the step slow as need summons

He knows, this shuttered being
without learning   he culls his black
hours   presses them well
                    to hunt
to find his seeking

How I would be some night-creature of God

At the Edge
18.2.67

this
ocean tougher than anything
(Spicer said
            and he saw right
this humiliating water
not a rhythm but consonant
erosion of myself
unpausing
overriding my little here
here the waste
of the sullen part

my body catches full
the rush
and comes once more
to understand
the baptismal force of death
                in this place

*

sometimes I see children
moving counter to the sound
and their cries overcome
the ringing cold
        I do not wish
        to be them again
        having passed with relief
        their cruellest joy

*

sometimes I see lovers cryptic
the eyes lovers have
secret with mirth at their invention
        I do not wish to
        be like them
        but I light candles
        at their windows

*

sometimes I see the poets
moving in through mist the blank
sun catching their shadow like tomorrows
        Donne and Hopkins and Garcia Lorca
        against the anguished face of Spicer
numbs my face with wind
as I reach to receive
their drowned steps by the fog

I will wish
to be of them
the lost souls who draw sea
maidens' songs like rubies
from the dark offshore caverns
the obedient solitaries who pray
a terror of vision
the long runners
dying exhausted ultimate in the cry

I will   be of them
these lonely who walk at the edge

—Ocean Beach, San Francisco

That Is Tad

the almost tuneless treble
measures me not less
knowingly because his hands
are new

he calls me   *Sister Mary!*
          and laughs when
my fingers find his

and I am his   sister
his younger
          for he teaches
me to play with love
as touched tendrils of sun

I hold Tad as
one borrowed for the day
a strange delight in
austered arms

          so I would bless him to sing
                    for me

within the grace of his sweet now
the songs of his joyous flight
always away   and forever to the gold

Among the Lions Night Is Still

the cough dyed heavy
stays the wrapped air
serves to seal the corners
of imagined movement
even the prey has abandoned
to various black wills

the seed sleeps unresting in the loins
waits for the first awe the glance of color crushed
that power of the great leap
coiled dark within the belly
feeds information to the blood
timed to countered heat of its course

the flat land lies humped beneath
the drawn pause between
light and light   where unlight
becomes the only living breath
seething taut creatures who increase
who devour the shapes of man and beast

and through metallic pulses
charged by the taste of sense
we listen with heads turned beyond solitary prides
we animals   caught in electric muscle

listen
listen
listen
        for the apocalyptic dawn

8 May 1967

the first face of light
is sharp with waking
is set like eyes
into the hill

and all the spiky shadows lie
at perfect random

phonepoles   mailboxes
stretch warm as cats
cars spring from kerbs
like cocker spaniels
newspapers wait for the bus
talk back the creased and coined tongue

before the windows bruise with
hammered hours
before the fearful refuse blows
dredging along the dull of streets

now when we can taste day
                in the air

alive at our sensual deity
we shall gather flowers   you and I
                and we shall gather
                        flowers

The Poets of Peace and Gladness

into gathered movement   love
measured   prodigal in
sound the tension of truth
patterns sacramentals

what is our peace but
harmonies counterpointed in form
                          of grace
songs
        in the communion gift
to make glad the sullen
laughter of sad hands

and draw skeins
of lighted tongues
burning their notes as candles
                  to the night

ROBERT LAX

KA-

LYM-

NI-

AD

-

PART

II

-

call it a crescent
crescent of rock

an island facing east

on a choppy sea

its silver
domes

its many
colored
fronts

a rock:
what grows on it?

a little
green
in win-
ter

the men with their blue nets
gri gri
out every night

& mending
the nets

in the
morning

the others who
go out
for months
at a time

& dive
(for

sponges)
the women who
weave

the women who
tie the hooks

to the long
white
lines

- - -

as though
he were
standing

under-
neath

the
sea

his eyes,
alive,
regarded

what swam
toward

him

what is
your work,

i ask-
ed

him

(with
his
hand)

he
made
a

dive

-

as flow-
ers draw
frag-
rance

from the
earth

their
speech

is pull-
ed
out
dai-
ly

from
this

rock

- - -

they
bang

they
bang

as
though
they
were
build-
ing

as
though
they
were
build-
ing

a
lad-
der

to
heav-
en

-

what
is this
board

this
wagon

this
sled

that
scores

along

the

rock

?

- - -

does
all
speech
turn
to
song

as
it
flies
up-
ward

?

does
ever-
y

is-
land

sing

all
night

all
day

?

does
all
speech
turn
to
song

?

does
ever-
y

is-
land

sing

?

does
all
speech
turn
to
song

all
night

all
day

?

Novel/

1.

oh
well

(she
con-
soled
her-
self)

some-
thing
good
is
bound
to
hap-
pen
(I'll
die)

&
go
to
heav-
en

which
has
al-
ways

sound-
ed

so
love-
ly

or
to
hell
which
sounds
even
worse

2.

why
does-
n't
any-
one

ever
die
&
go
to

(new-
port)

?

3.
sud-
den-
ly

she

real-
ized

that
there
was-
n't

a
resort

in
the
world

she
want-
ed

to
go
to

any-
way

so
that
was
that

ETHEL LIVINGSTON

Legend of the Waving Lady

I

Wind break on the beach
She's waving
One arm dark on the sky
Like a bare branch on the sky
Calling

It was fall
The leaves had come down in town
Like summer curtains stored for spring
And the summer boats were docked
Like plastic toys put up.

He was tall
With long brown fingers
Hard on the stiff threads of the rope
With the yellow of fall
Straining with
The curve of the sail.

Wind break on the beach
Out past the point of land
Where the fingers of jetty
Crawl out
She's waving
One arm against the sky

Force
On the sail
Out
Where the water breaks
Till the wood splinters on the rock
Like a match stick snapping
Between teeth.

Wind broke on the beach.

II

She was beautiful
But she died waiting
For the boats to come back   cursing
The men who went out in the fall
When the red leaves came down.

Now she stands where the water breaks white
With one hand raised to
Shadow her eye
Waving
        to the boats
        to the rock

III

Laughingly
He told me the legend once
Before

And afterward I watched him
Move down the beach
Bending his long brown hands
Into fists
Climbing into the boat

It was fall and
The summer boats were docked
Like plastic toys put aside

Wind break on the beach
Where the spars hang
On the rock
And the yellowness has turned grey
And wet on the sand

She's waving
With one arm high on the sky

Wind break on the beach.

Postcard: Two Figures from an Oriental Print

They are walking
    like two people caught
    in a passageway   somewhere else.
    a man and a horse

    not quite an imitation they
    are a parallel dimension
    of movement through a perfect space —
    brown rimmed by a quarter
    inch of white.
    cardboard.

    still

    out of flatness
    the gray of the horse —
    the curve of the back into haunches
    while the white blurr of belly
    swells soft
    behind angular shoulders   the man
    leading
    with shoes on the edge
    of the page

bound by postmarks
to a day   they are
still walking
toward some point
under your finger tip that
you can never touch.

"Unending sameness of questionable quality."

"Unending sameness of questionable quality."
That's what the lady said,
That's what I heard.
Perhaps she was talking about the
      milk trucks that leave at six
      o'clock and rattle in the early air,
Or about the shiny grease in the
      copper pan, the bacon fat.
Or maybe it was the instant coffee
      can that was never full, even
      when it hadn't been opened
Or the orange and yellow dress with
      the ink stain on the shoulder
      and a cigarette burn on the hem.
But maybe she was talking about
      something more ethereal—
      the constant search for an intangible
      god who would never find his way
      into a pulpit,
Or the significance in the daily ringing
      of the twelve o'clock bells.
It could have been that, or
      the torn sheet
            or
            the blue detergent

                        or
                the leather bag
        with a green strap
                        or the paint spot
                        on the couch.
She could have been talking about you and me,
But I don't think she was talking at all.
She saw a crack in the ceiling
And you don't talk about cement
                or
                wood putty
                or
                scotch tape,
                        you know.
You just hope they will hold.

they are closing in.

I

they are closing in.
the trees are making a dark green tent
that is stifling me.

i am breathing in the heavy scent of
pine needles.
i am choking.

II

i want to brush aside the branches
and pick up a small pebble.
i will give it to him
and walk away to the sea.

III

i want to step on the knees of the beach
and let the salt wash over my feet.

i want to put my knees next to the sand
and let the water wash over my thighs.

let there be grey light.
i do not want the sun to show my skin.
i am my own god of fortune.
i am my own god.
i will pardon myself.

IV

let me dissolve into the grey.
let me escape into the sky
on the wings of a dead day.
i would be born again
to a second life.

V

i would live on the shore this time
but there will be a faint smell
of pine about the neck of my shirt
to remind me
and i will have to go back.

Slow Rhythm—

Slow Rhythm—
     an oiled motion of dark thighs
     and drunken castanets and
     high-heeled boots—snapping against
     the splintered wooden floor.

Somehow you know when it arrives,

Somehow you know when it arrives,
There's just one day when it's
                              there.
You get up
    out of wrinkled sheets
And you're hot because the heat
    is on and it's cold outside—
Not fall cold but
              cold.
There's a grey capping the day,
But the air is light underneath
    and cold and sharp
    like an aluminum ice tray.
It's cold
      to touch.
It rained last night—
                  wet
                     rain
And the leaves fell,
                some of them
                lots of them,
So the ground looks
    like a shadow of the tree above—
A mirror reflection,
    but the color is
                  real and thick
                        and heavy
Because they're leaves
And you know what wet leaves are like.
There are leaves on the wet cement too—
    red and yellow and brown
    and brown and yellow
    and green and yellow

and brown.
They're like footsteps.
They stick
        to the grey cement
Because they're wet too.
If you pick one up
      it's like wet paper with a stem.
They're dying.
You know tomorrow they'll
      dry up and blow away
      and the yard man
      will rake them and burn them
                    red
                    and
                    yellow
                    and
                    brown.
But when they blow away
      there's an impression
      on the grey cement
And when you try to smudge it with your toe
It won't smudge.
Anyway
      like I said
You know when winter comes—that one day
And then
         you only have to wait
         til the rest of the leaves fall
         and the rain turns white
         and the yard man goes inside.
Then everyone else will know too.

DICK LOURIE

The WhenIwas

(*from* "Calls on the Dream Telephone")

"How are you boy
my right leg's worse today
the eyes blur, pain expected
cooler tomorrow in some spots
I'm ninety-four, you know"

On purpose he called
just at Pushup-Time every night
kept sounding better, too.
The night I was down to ten per
he slipped and said ninety-three

I knew I had him then
ran him into Public Welfare
"For the Good For the Good" they told him
put him kindly to sleep
we shook hands all round

then I ran home and did thirty

The Bestfriend

(*from* "Calls on the Dream Telephone")

Still dripping, I grabbed it
"Yes I'm healthy
No I don't want a story"
I knew who it was.
Always when I'm in something important

Back in the tub
the boats had nearly sunk
Complete Works was under water

I cried and cried
and kicked out the bathroom walls

Naked and bigger than everyone
I ran away
couldn't get dry either
so I jumped in the nearest phonebooth
but I'd never answer it

crying and crying like a baby

Ann's House

when my house is full of flowers the brightness
is better than sun: when afternoons
are long shadows in the east rooms
violets glow in the near darkness   a red
rose opens like the sound of a lute   but
winters they all sleep and wait   white
white are the April beds

Rink

The man in the yellow sweater who will
take no crap from anyone and wears a
tight face on a wrinkled head pushes past
us to the smooth wood floor and as the lights
fade   as the organ sputters and calls out
like an ecstatic thing to the men   on
the run he takes his place in the circling
dance   the long dance   the fast dance of the men.
As a piece of light he dances   lifts in
unnameable slight gesture his black skate
leans and taps his own silent clean music
sheds fat lays   weak beer   and moves to music.

"english"

If she stood with you where the men playing
bocce roll the wood ball so it thumps on
the hard sand then twisting aim their bodies
like tight dancers along the subtle planned
invisible line it must cleave to to
win   would she then at last know why you in
that double-jointed fear of telling her
and not telling her will sit hours over
coffee   sometimes pressing your hands around
the hot cup   and not look at her   and then
touch her long hair like some affectionate
brother or old man   never what you are?

the Hitler Dwarf

this morning   though I had heard about him
from my friends I saw for the first time the
Hitler Dwarf   whistling and striding up to
me through the dirty snow piles alongside
Seventh Avenue   the short solid legs
slightly bent   the familiar mustache   a
brown trenchcoat almost to the ground   he said

in passing "are you out looking for sharp
images?   too early   even your girl
is still in bed   dreaming of you   in fact
no-one's up yet   but wait   pretty soon when
the sun's out and the snow melts   if you will
meet me someplace for coffee we can discuss our plans as to the future of the race"

The Madman Looks at His Fortune

The radiator knocked and hissed
and at the third cut
the fat deck split me
the ace of spades late
one night.

So I said: "I would hope
love gets here first
for at least a few shakes
one or two groans and whispers
while it is still light"

and stared at the flat card
trying to recall some twinge
around the heart. All I could think of
was names of women
whose phones had been disconnected

until with a sharp crack
that pointed black rose
exploded into flower
over my eyes. Death's
no feeling, doesn't make a noise

is only a sweet smell.

The Madman Goes to a Party

First I ritual
myself (naked) clean as fire
in my shower hot
as fire, scrubbed
(thinking of her face)

And I rub dry
this one body I have
the big blue towel wraps
unwraps me (I have decided
finally not to hide

How shall I dress up to meet her
good new lover formally?
I think my pink paunch
cowboy hat and a long knife
sheathed, on my leather belt

Of course I'll shave
under my arms
brush my teeth and shake hands
but he can't call me
by my nickname.

And with her
even if she's polite
or brings me refreshments
I won't speak   I won't eat
till just before I leave

then I'll say "how's your new lover?"

Two Fish Cosmologies

I

from the end of a thin string taped on my ceiling
a red and yellow paper fish hangs

when I breathed in his mouth round as a kiss
his skin   transparent   a globe   a window
crinkled out   grew rounder

now when the light shines on him his shadow is
orange   he turns in the warm evening
air   with slow joy
like an old planet

a vision: the room spins and I see a
thousand years pass   nobody's in
the room   in the evening   warm currents

cross one another
still and slow in his
joy circling
he moves full
he moves
full
of my breath

II

hanging down from the flat
speckled canvas   the fish
of the world turns
on his string   history
is in his belly.

while he's crumpling and
chewing you up like paper
you could get a chance to peer out
on the fat open mouth,
you'd see some stars
leap and explode   you would find
out how his breath stinks

and once I even saw
reflected off of the flat night
my own face   pocked with joking
sour with lust   then Zip!   he swallowed   and
things got
dark again.

in the master bedroom of the white house

in the master bedroom of the white house
is a mirror as tall as a man in
a heavy gilt frame at the foot of the
bed: it's here the president has to stand
naked to scratch his sores or to squeeze his
pale belly between his hands—do you think

he's so different from ourselves as we
consider before climbing into our
beds at night the war's progress bulletins
or the magazine picture of that child
naked   alive   face melted and body
burned like meat by stuff dropped from American planes—look—   as we yawn   what's left of that
mouth works   doing a parody of speech:

"Mr. President   Fellow Citizens
look in *this* mirror   love your body   kiss it

Two Birthday Poems

I

in the dream your face appeared in a blue light
the open mouth screamed "you shit   leave me alone"
as hard as I could I hit you with my fist
your nose broke open   the blood breaking from it
in waves became the light   in such red light you
were healed   your body was made visible   I
opened up my hands   we embraced and there made
love   weeping so much our tears became light   such
a clear light we lay in it until morning.

II

the first time I slept with you in the same bed
I saw you were having bad dreams   grinding your
teeth in sleep I could not get to
                                        as if in
the desert you were lying beneath Rousseau's
white moon knowing the lion stood over you
and afraid to open your eyes   like the child
you told me about who thought what scared her could
not get at her if she closed her eyes
                                        but I
know you feel even in sleep this lion's breath—
animal face against your face he waits for
your eyes to open   he is roaring at you
now "love love"   now he is whispering "love".

CLIVE MATSON

Today

    another irresistible force,
have to swing with it.
                Heavy clouds &
I wait for the tables to turn
                    or push it a little,

she's trying to be a bigger martyr
than me:
          sick, tired, world against her—
    see if
she can transmit her sex & junk yens,
get me to nurse her pain away

and somehow I'm in the same groove,
Mutual Competing Martyr Complex!
                   Groan
and clutch my liver,
try going one worse &
             set off a tiny pressure bomb
inside her skull so
her face opens with concern
              and she does it all
with brown hair tickling my belly,
               well I'd be
    breast fed and sucked off.

Drink Wine in the Corner Store,

talk with strangers and fence
with friends,
      walk for hours.

Meditate east by the black shiny river
rustling in the dark,

later go where
rods are rapping up the street for kicks
or tough lust or sweet love,

dig the swaying shoulders & swinging hips,
hooded
        eyes, glamour hounds
and masked faces by neon,
                        cruise and
turn away the wanting eyes.

Compare old lovers' thighs to hers,
brown Winston on 7th Street, Julie
on hillsides and on car seats, blonde
Martha in her mother's bed.

Back into the despair groove
20,000 years old and tired of it,
everyone's as sad as me
                        and wants the same,

                        now in the
empty room double clutch again &
reach for the gear smooth flowing
above the changing rumbles.

                        Flowered curtains
dusky brown in the lamplight, cigarette butts
with lipstick smears in the ashtray,
rumples on the bed where she sat with
legs sideways and talking in
                        honeyed voice or
whining like she does,
                ah I want to open
        her throat
                or my own maybe,
        or both.

I want my woman
and she's out somewhere in the night
            with odds I couldn't figure
gossiping with a joint between her fingers
or flirting or letting off steam,

the witchwoman not under my finger:
slyly turned away so her hair would
light with flame again &

these pictures I'd push away or
                        not believe though
jealousy is a function of love and
so is possessiveness,
                the same old fate &
hope will come with the dawn, too.

The woman here maybe,
                lush Venus or stupid girl
a figure in poses around accepting trust
if I want her alive
                for new games in the
clear mirrors of the mutual dig
with current in the spine and
                        light in the brain.

I Watch

        The Hustler, it's over
                & I walk out
        to lights on the street.

                        Cross over

                                        Oh
                        Are my chains gone,

```
        Lady Luck, is
This your lily breath?
                Night air!
                            Blow thru me
                        as I cruise   to
    What dark doorway that keeps
                            my Lover?
    Wink
            ,green light
        didja show me
a sign,
        Is it for red Love
                        between my legs?
        & the pink Cobra?
```

Against Jealousy.

Well Babe I'd die almost
without you & I know
you'd feel the same but

I'll shrivel up without some
new young love &
                    today I saw
your blue eye roving.

We'll get along, maybe better
if you'll let me loose &
when I'm late coming home

ask me no questions and I'll
treat you the same.
                    And cross
fingers jealousy don't
clench teeth or slam doors &

tear us apart.

Vision: Second Psalm.

God is returned to Earth.
                            Watch Him swirl amid
stars & infinite whirling galaxies &
                                    invisibly descend
to walk among His strange animals
from the sea.
                    We suck Him down with the vacuum grown
huge between our minds' ambition &
                                    our poor destiny,
now overwhelmed with too many ancestors before us
all with smaller parts.
                        Who covered the planet with four
walls for many and soon all.
                            A private freaking chamber
or palace for our dreams &
nothing left but
                    each other. We live on the brink of
destruction as always
                        only now by our own hand.
God smiles & chuckles in the cold sky,
                                    thru the walls---
I've picked up His word & can't put Him down.
Hung with Him
                    in the dark room where I live with music &
beer or liquor or lie drugged,
                            jack off or dream.
                            Mostly I care how I feel.
            The last 15 years
spent trying to get used to myself.
                                Not much luck.
        All the dreams of some holy grail. How I've worked
to unite body and mind
                        as if they aren't the same.
& so by sleight of hand I put you on big,
                                    out on the street

jive or get fucked in some routine or fuck someone or
walk silent in tension
                        withholding dreams, sad or happy &
watch around me the renaissance
                        of the newly unsuppressed
mostly unknown behind busy eyes,
                        the women stuck up w/
                                        men,
cats out of one bag looking for another &
the dawning wonder in some eyes
                        ---until Earth the great
spinning stone grinds us to dust:
                        you can do what you want.
            & master fate a little
each woman like a queen & each man like a king.

Full Swing Circus.

Walk down the street,
                        sun shwonk
on the left,
shadows to my right.
                        Palms and cheeks
caress the light breeze,
                        this cool air
blowing clear thru the stratosphere
around the world.

Wrap around me the high birds' song,
        soot spice in my nose,
whoosh/drone of natural jets above—
                                chrome flash
in the sun
+ diesels' blat-rattle,
                        I'm high on the world.

The full swing circus moves
around me,

           red and green sparkles/
desire and fear an elastic bubble
I'm holding in a sphere
                          while
things ask attention and

I'll pick out a colored scene
stretching the bubble to a slick window and
flip
     a little for pleasure

careful never to jar anchor chain loose
or lose touch on balance—
gyroscopes spinning in the cells,
bring my mind to its senses
                        and the worlds there.

I walk on green mountain tops,
        through brown ocean deeps,
swim in the tree postcards,
        through tenement blues.
Fondle the brown skin girls
        among tropical fruit,

dig a little here,
                    a little there,
dig a little everywhere.

While somewhere
head hunters stumble behind me
                          sniffing
and high tailers frolic beside me,
the diggers and the dug.

The sun-shwonked going for a meadowlark:
beads, flowers, incense and smiles
                        sprawling on the grass,

the brown spider weaving his taut nets
between green grass lovers,
                                        the grass-hopper
trying to be a head.

The head humming with jewels and evil flowers,
the butterfly pad hopping,
                                        the hand circlers
touching bodies with kaleidoscope eyes,

Kirk in poverty and hunger laying his way
across the nation.
                        Lovey's in the hot state,
                    Debbie's living in unlove,
Alex stranded on the plains,
Noah entombed in Brooklyn long ago
with churning dreams.

The old style cocooned comfort babe is everywhere dying,
the new style the dynamo now!
since I'm alive I'll suck life's juices
                                        and
I'll find its juices eyes open in the near chaos,

man coming out of the dark ages to where
life is a high and drugs a way there.

Life's a weird trip and I
pick up and reel in the twisty lines
                                        between people,
        high voltage at the connections.

High tension at crossed wires,
the lines burnt out by shorts
and bodies pushed apart,
                                        the lines fusing
together or separate again,
the process repeating as

we make the world our playground
                              in the rich slime,
          in afternoon sunlight,
          in faint moonlight,
          in green leaflight

where talk is soul honey and
voices gold on the highest plateau.

The impossible two-way developed,
the charges equalizing as bodies
gently stir warm fluids
                    and the tingling flowers
cunt and cock rise full or shrivel again,
tune out the riot/
              dodge the humans:

there are so many buzzing around the heights
who've forgot their altitude
and the depth of their despair.

          The walls will close in again,
the sky will splinter and
the evil night come,
                    the district of pain close by,
quick step and look behind.

You come through the rough road and into the postcards
watching the movie along magic street
knowing the props will collapse and expose another scene,
                                        this scene
iridescent water magicking the rocks beneath.
Shifting shapes and rich color
among preying monsters too,

freeze the life/spectrum at patterns, pictures,
reverberations and the next love touch.

In the dark night I'll tune in
the heavy zonk layer or the acceptance layer,
in the day the light magic layer.

JASON MILLER

First Note

Night enters the skin's pores.
It is time. In those same holes
broken of bead-sweat, now a curtain

blows, flaps, and an evening sea
is waved. Winds chill and gulls
quiet in cluster under dock and eaves.

On far-out waves picked with moonlight
an emerald-green somewhere is playing.
A place hearkens that is windless.

O island, is it the first tree—it
so awkwardly holds to its branches,
protective of my gaze? Shore

drying at my feet. Leaf, the road
in your green palm inhales my space.
Blue gods are bridging in weed.

A mountain piercing its breath touches
the bottom of the sea, sounds...

Garden! Peaks woken
in the resounding of ignited stars,
and blood dreaming in roses.

The Solitary

And cells in breaking

converge. In lifting
into a head, are breaking,
are pealing sounds of slightest
motion, manipulation by

unknown hands of a rubber
in the bones, and wind
feeding at the flesh.

Cells of a house,
of a room, of a family,
separating into the lines
of flowers. Silences

group amidst diminishing
words, and a dilating of
shapes veil an oncoming

monkey skull. A weight of
suitcases unknotting a red
pain in the back. A burning.

Multiplying rain of one
stone lifting a face

and he looks in song.

Blind Man

                    Casual
turning to a window. Passengers
noting his coming, quick
in their glance. A looking
not acknowledged. He moves

down the aisle, is
steered to a seat by
hands. A duty done. A
breathing come easier. The
bus moves on. But there is no
view at the window. His

being there. Here. In the
early morning. With a lunchbag
also. The glances dart. His
eyes like mine. A clothing wearing

of itself, of an approaching sand
color, scaliness of wrinkles,
stains. Away they turn. A
whistling. Going in his ears.
"It is because they watch me
that I am different."

Blossom

Into my shoulder your head bores
a rock of beginning sleep helplessly
heavily making a space. On my chest

your rested hand a hammer. Hair
wandering the face of our skin
touches bones in the weight of curled

wetnesses. Darkly
without feature our bodies luxuriate
a last time in sinking nourishment

and ride out of the lasting sweetness.
Dryly our legs untangle a meadow
of weeds. I shiver in your sweat.

In the sleep of your closed eyes
movement has returned, an undulation.
Is a dream starting?

A purple vein twitches in your bit neck.

The Constancy

And the soil was not refused.

In the blind ache of her steadily
moving fingers,
         bell-threads touched,
and a mother knows the dreaded
moment patient work has cupped.
The vigil over.
         This was not her life.
Her mouth formed with pain. A breath
choked, she cannot utter. And is done,
her hands leaving go a running child.

In a new coldness
         she drapes her head
and shoulders in a shawl
and is somewhere
         glimpsed now among
dark trees or in a spring
twilight alongside the tall crops.
And the vigil is not over.
         A fine rain
of dust she leaves at her son's
window. It is her only weeping
as she watches
         him tripping on the stars
around his feet, eyes of yellow hair,
spiraling to clouds.

Step

There is no last step.

It is not the end to lower
your foot a step you cannot
feel. Lowering it farther,
farther, a tension of balance.

Where, the landing of this step?

Blindly the foot going in the one
knowledge of a widened gap.
Knees bending
               and nothing there

but the motion being made
is made, the body
backward lowering itself
and the heart opened in
fear, in daring,   catches
a grass light, catches
an air's breath
while the body plunges

black hope

birthing the stone
nothing will touch.

(Square in Savannah)

The morning answers. In
its open palm a lily eats.

Pigeons alight on rocks over
the dark worms. Bobbing in hunger,

in ritual. Twigs return to the sun
dry, brittle. The dew descends.

At the top of trees soil
is transplanted in blue fruit.

And the cricket's shadow lengthens
in a voice under the tree. Listen!

The grasses are bending. Foam-green
extending their tips. Like shoreless

waves. A step articulating.
Uncrashing. In the wind. A blade

slaps a bird's feet. Blade and feather
lying on a note in the tower.

Summer Night

Straightly sliced half-moon.
Line of darkness.

A white Congregational Church
illuminated from floodlights in the grass.

Cars pass. Flickers of radio music.
Empty sidewalks.

Street dark with houses.
Down, window blinds into horizontal waves.

Across a pond decomposing stenches.
Bushes of water plants yellow in moonlight.

Branches drooping in heavy foliage,
a measuring stillness of leaves.

Sloop-lash! A frog's
muddy hands turning a fan.

Fire Song

Coming into a circle
lower than earth, than sea,

the rim of a gold ring, do not grasp
it, it is moving out into the folds
of a standing figure who slowly
in its warmth does not see it,

looking in the fuel of his body,
the crackling of its parts, blossoms
held out in the prayer of rain,

flaming cup of flame

And the earth of web-feet
duck-paddle a way of water,

vein-roots sending into chasms
a flush of turned sea

And fired limbs helplessly
in the dance are spread like grass

the hold of a rhythm, each in time.

DOUG PALMER

My people,

My people,
it is
to you
I am
as God
and
yourselves.
Let it
come
forth
first
from myself,
then
then
from
yourselves.
My people,
I am
loving you
each to each
as you
are
here.
I love
you.
I am
here
to the quiet
to the burst
of my
push
and
help
I am
come

to myself
yes
first
but only
to you.
O people
we are
on the
first
heart
of the matter,
the first
colors
in the
pain,
the
first
help
for
this taste
of O
honey
on your
tongue
or your
first
lips,
if you
like
that
taste.
But that
shall not be
by me
thrust on

you.
Your taste,
as you
can.
But honey,
is the bee,
is the sting,
and is life
gone
out.
O honey
honey
is the
time
that we
have
now
that we
today
and today
shall be
martyrs,
for our
people.
O the
cause
is
now.
Even as
I am
a poet,
I am
a
picket.
O people,
I am
picketing

for
this
thing
which
is
when a
man comes up
to another,
and like
he was
himself yes
but
himself only.
Treats him
as a man
regardless
of
difference.
It is coming
O my
people
it is
on us
on us
on us
in us
up to us
and I
love you
to give
everything
for
it.
Every thing
of
feeling.
O

love
my people
is
all

about
us.
Today.

In a field

In a field
big enough
for so many
there were
          dancing
these poor
          people
dancing
saying their
          prayers
dancing
and I
was one of
          them.
Hundreds
I tell you.
I can't tell
you
what I mean.
I join hands
with all these
          people
and I don't
          know
most of them.
With my wife
          Ruth
and our son

          Tad
we'll go there
someday
and find
a lot more people
than we'd thought
were there.
Dancing
we'll dance.
There may
finally only be
the three of
          us
there.
Walking together
saying what
          then
we'll say.
Running
or laughing
or lying panting
from
          running.
We are in on
something.
We sense it.
We feel the air
faster near us.

We walk back
to each other.
What else
is there
to dance
     to
in a field?
What if
suddenly
you understand
each other
     better
going back.
What was
in the field
was grass
and earth
and us three
and
better for it.
Some days
all poor people
find their

fields
open to
the wind
and coming across
they lie down
in the flat
of the field
and don't
forget
where they are.
Lie down
and don't forget
they'll get
     up.
Lying in no
shade but that
thrown by the grass.
They will lie there
imagining themselves
no different.
My love is like
     that.

Clap hands

Clap hands
together
to feel
in your hair
its softness.
To feel
in the evening
we're getting up
bright and
early

to stay home
to each other.
Or early
to go some place,
a ride
in the blue
sky overhead,
and the trees
pointedly.
And the ground

soon
we'll find grass
on and roll
in it.
And
lie out to
the sun,shading
the eyes,
this can
be like
your hand in
mine.
Feeling

the river water
cold till
you're in a while,
then the sun
so fine on
my shoulders,
and today,
no breeze,so
no sand
on me.
Warm,
in the sun.

High tide, and

I

High tide,and
the city policeman
in his car
along the rail.

II

As in your
back pocket,different
                colored
wads of toilet tissue,
homes you've visited,
and friends.

III

And if you
were walking

on the railroad track,
your hands
spinning backwards,
sideways toward him,
and he hollered
something,and you fell,
together laughing,
sitting there,you
could wish he had a cold,
so you could give him
some toilet paper
for blowing his nose.

IV

And yet
he'll go his way,
and you'll maybe,
also,hoping that
he will,and

not be there
if the thing is done,
he must be there for.

animal in both hands
to be lifted,
with regrets.

V

Stray things
in his way,
like the hurt

VI

Give him
the direction of
picked roses.

These poems,

These poems,
though they
propose,
are not
just what
the world
is.
     /How they
fail,you
shall answer,
as you go
beyond them.
As you shall.
As you
must.
          For the
world comes
last in your
life.After
all
is said,
then you
must do.
And doing,
the new

poems
come out,
must be
held up to
the light,
and eventually
even they
that are
best,
fail.
          Because
the world
is too much
for them,
for the eyes
that hold
in their sway
your passing.
Even so,
you can't
help but
love
them.
For your
eyes

even so
must have
images
and cast up
new flotsam,
and call
that
new insight.
And expect
a new
tide.
    And hold
the wood
to a fire,
any fire,
and tell
is it green
enough
to maintain
itself,
smoldering.
And if not,
all you can
hope
is
some few
things in

you
call forth
goodness
and
mercy,
as you
give these.
And this
will last.
And new
growth,
in the
wilderness,
in the
unstrewn beach,
the pushing tide
up over the rocks,
up over the
low-tide
things.
And if that
isn't love,
a form,
you must
describe it
right.

MARGE PIERCY

Why the soup tastes like the Daily News

The great dream stinks like a whale gone aground.
Somewhere in New York Harbor
in the lee of the iron maiden
it died of pollution
and was cast up on Cape Cod by the Provincetown Light.
The vast blubber is rotting.
Scales of fat ripple over the waters
until the taste of it
like a sulphur yellow factory of chemical plenty
dyes every tongue.

Rain falls on Ioannina

Grey clouds sink.
All day from my hotel room
I watch the grey lake rise.
I rub and blow on my inkstained fingers
awkward in my joints
patient as that wading stork.
Fog creeps in the window.
Smoke spools out.
From the cracked egg
of looted synagogue
weeds sprout in the rain.
In the glass and concrete orphanage
girls are learning to weave rugs
to sell to tourists.
It is not so bad, they say.
The soldier said the same,
hitchhiking toward his village
of rocks and gnarled shepherds,
about the army. The equipment

is new and American.
The army is a major industry
as under the Turks,
as under the Germans.
I am American and a tourist.
I am learning something about wet
and grey and bad.

Now all at once it is colder

You talk too much.
Like a film run backward your day gallops by
and you rush on as if interruptions would tear you.
You are burning, burning
dry and hot and sudden as a parched weed.
The flash blinds you.
You hear only the crackling of your flesh
and the amphetamine rhythms of your own voice.
Your arm feels hard as varnish to my hand.
Come back, I say,
and you answer, Come with me. Hurry!
I say, I don't want to go there.
Hurry, hurry, you shout, we're leaving now!
A cinder blows in my eye.
A smell of singed wool makes me sneeze.
The last thing to fade
is the copter's whir of your voice still calling.
Did I listen hard enough?
what were you trying to say?
I think it was Goodbye.
I think it sounded like Help me.
It could have been, Give me your hand, hold on please.
But all I could hear in the fizzing and crackling was Hurry!
                                        Hurry!
and I saw no reason to hurry, then.

Song of the nudge

There are eight people in this room.
I am in love with five of them
besides myself whom I love only sometimes.
The other is a girl I do not know.
The other is a man who has been walking off slowly for
months.
I shout, he turns his head
he can hear nothing and sees only grimaces.
I am loving five of them
whether they like it or not and often they don't.
It is being hopped by an electric windmill with cowbells,
a rain of salamanders and feather beds and overripe onions.
It is a sweaty tango with a python
among the marshmallow bushes, I know it.
Today two of these people filmed a girl with a smile
trying to give dollars or flowers to passersby
who ducked their heads and hustled on.
There is no love without its coercion,
there are no gifts without taxes, all sparrows know.
Nothing belongs to me except my hands
and I go around trying to give them away.
A spare hand in the house, nasty, curious as a monkey
you couldn't keep it in a cage. what would it eat?
it would probably break things.
it is probably better to lock the door.

Embryos

1. Wee

I am thin as nail parings. Light as dandruff.
When I cry I listen to myself
pages of Bible paper turning over.

Who will love my morning toadstool sighs?
My rubbery lusts sway like sea anemones.
My hatreds mew once and stifle, still blind.

I will zip my mouth and put mittens on my hands
and innocent and eggstill I will wait.
On a teatray my vanilla prince will come.

2. *Whey*
Why do you cry? No one comes.
I am waiting in the grey to be born.

Your legs are driftwood
your face is a pike's
your touch rusts.
Why do you rub the mirror?
How could my hair thin when no one pulled it?
whose fingers pressed in my cheeks?
what mousemouth sucked my breasts?
My shadow limps from the window baaing.
Fog is in me.

Who are you crying for? Ash
in the chimney flue.
The sun to fatten my shrunk shadow.
Quick, bear me: my gourd chest shakes.
The clock trickles sand on my forehead.
I am dry as onions.

See the sun's fatherly eye
opening to heat me.
Today is my right birthday.
                    Bury her.

Apologies

Moments
when I care about nothing
except an apple:
red as a mapletree
satin and speckled
tart and winey.

Moments
when body is all:
fast as an elevator
pulsing out waves of darkness
hot as the inner earth
molten and greedy.

Moments
when sky fills my head:
bluer than books
cleaner than number
with a wind
fresh and sour
cold from the mouth of the sea.

Moments
of sinking my teeth
into now like a hungry fox.
Never otherwise
am I so cruel:
never otherwise
so happy.

Vil for the layman

On the sunblasted and sterile island of Vil
inhabited by gulls and goats, as is well known
stone tumuli stand among the gorsebushes
carved outside with goatheads and winged stallions,
inside sometimes with great stone women, sometimes
slim boys and fishfaced serpents (lightning symbols).

Gold filigree work of great finesse was found
and deplorably looted by early expeditions.
Inscriptions on stone tablets reveal a language
compared with Greek and Hittite unprofitably.
Fiore's recent translations too proved fraudulent.

A high civilization brought to its downfall
by a plague, invasion, drouth, shifting trade routes,
effete sex practices, or prolonged civil war,
earthquake, fire or religious suicide.
In any event, all here are dead except
the tourists, the souvenir venders and the goats.

By the throned Mothers suckling lambs or infants
Fasolis shows the Mediterranean base.
From words transliterated by his patented method
Sir Stafford Rumford Coates has proved to many
the Indo-European source (viz. deoz for god).
Research under auspices of the East Orange New Jersey
University using computers and carbon dating
is establishing precise cultural strata.

In the meantime a picture of the reconstructed
national costume (barebreasted) and a popular account
of prenuptial rites of transsocial participation,
serial cohabitation and the socalled 'goat dances'
depicted in certain wall murals, have received
adequate coverage in all Western news media.

Book of the Month has distributed *Vēnus of Vil*
and film rights sold for an unprecedented fee.

A Hilton Hotel of thirty stories, Playboy keyclub
and jet airstrip are nearing completion none too soon.
The international elite initially attracted
by poet X. Albert's rhapsody *Salt, Sun and Goat
Dance: Vil!* proclaiming the isle the dionysiac navel
have found it spoiled: and indeed upon
the right tit of the fattest recumbent mother goddess
is carved Kansas, a date, and the message Mirnie Sucks.

For Jeriann's hands

When I hug you you are light as a grasshopper.
your bones are ashwood the Indians used for bows
you bend and spring back and can burn the touch,
a woman with hands that know how to pick things up.
You sit on a chair with your booted feet thrust forward
and drink bourbon like a trooper or a little girl.
stiff as frozen rope the words poke out
lopsided, in a fierce clothespin treble.
You move with a grace that is all function
you move like a bow drawn taut and released.
sometimes your wrists are transparent.
sometimes an old buffalo man frozen on the prairie stares
                                     from your face.

Your hair and your eyes are the color
of creek running in the afternoon opaque under slanted sun.
Loyalties strike in you flint on flint.
you are warm as a baker's oven.
you are stubborn and hardy as a rubber mat.
you are light as a paper airplane and as elegant
and you can fly.

The secret of moving heavy objects is balance, you said
in a grey loft full of your sculpture   doors   mirrors
                                           windows
figures piercing or hung on those boundaries
leaping their thresholds/arms poked through but heads
                                             averted/
impaled on broken mirrors/ passing and gone.
Objects born from you are mended, makeshift.
their magic has to defy raw ends and nails sticking out,
their magic rides over rust and splinters,
over shards of glass and cellophane beginning to rip.
You and your poet are always moving.
fragments of your work litter the banks of minor highways.
shattered faces of your icons lie on Hoboken junkyards,
float as smog over the East River,
grow black with the dust of abandoned coalbins,
fall smashed from a truck on Manhattan Bridge, stopping
                                             traffic.
There is never money to rest.
there is never money to buy time or sleep or materials.
your hands work wood into desolate saints, not into dollars.

I remember the small rooms you made of wax
where people stood in taut ellipses staring and blind
with tenderness, with agony, with question and domestic
                                             terror.
Revelation shone through the wax bodies.
They were candles burning. on the floor as I slept
I knew they moved and had being in the dark.
you wanted to cast them in bronze but could not afford to.
The August sun melted them all.

The dancers you use in pageants burn too in the dark
moving with masks and machines and chairs that trot and
                                             wail
flimsy ragtag things that turn holy and dance

till there is no audience but all grope and stumble in your
world.
When you enter it is clear there is someone come,
no longer a woman, not highbreasted and wiry, not warm
quick flesh
but a makeshift holy artifact moving on the blank face of
the dark
as on a river: ark, artifact, dancer of your own long breaking
dance
which makes itself through you fiercely totally passing in
light
leaving you thin and darkened as burnt glass.

Homo faber: the shell game

Pyramids of flesh sweat pyramids of stone.
Each slave chiseled his cheap as dust life in rock,
with labor dragged from him he marked his own grave
heaped geometrically over the painted chrysallis.
The Roman slaves built stadia and roads for empire and
trade.
Cathedrals: parallel vaulted hands the color of winter clouds
where choirs of polyphonic light rise from chilly slabs
while nobles with swords on and skinny saints lie under the
floor.
Fortresses, dungeons, keeps, moats and walls.
Dwellings salon on salon set in gardens too vast for
strolling.
Skyscrapers where nobody lives filled with paper.
Where do the people live and what have they made for
themselves
splendid as these towers of glass, these groves of stone?
The impulse that in 1910 molded banks as temples,
where now does it build its central artifact?
The ziggurat, the acropolis, the palace of our dream
whose taste rings in the blood's cave like belladonna,

all scream in the eagle's preyseeking swoop of the bomber,
those planes expensive as cities, the sharklean submarines of
death,
the taut kinetic tower of the missile,
the dark fiery omphalos of the bomb.

ALEX RAYBIN

Titan's Lament

I have stolen the sun from the moon's black mouth
But not without some loss of innocence.
Be not against me Old Herodotus
For when the wind whistles among the silent winter oaks
A man must do
What a man must do.

I know only that in the dark
In the cool darkness
There came a voice unlike any I had ever...
And I was afraid.

The sun   is everything
It is more than the light
More than the image
Which chases oblivion from the edges of the world
Is the heart
Of the new embryo
Is life

But only as long as the waking moment does innocence
                                                    abide
In the presence of death
And to find
(in the moon's black shadow)
That the presence
Is real, indeed,
Relevant,
An essential part
Is....a disappointment.

I live in the midst of all
That is found in the shadow of the moon's black mouth

But I have stolen the sun.

The Conversation

We sat in the garden together. She said,
"What do you know of roses? Stamen. Stem.
Petal. Root. What do you know
Of the sadness of roses, the loneliness
Of roses? What do you know
Of the indescribable anguished isolation
Of the dying rose? The birds stop singing,
The flowers clutch their stalks
The earth itself cries out for its stricken daughter
And every living thing moans in its heart
For the death of the rose."

Much later the rain fell. She sat
In the rain. She sat silently. She sat
With her back to the sea, her eyeballs
Very white, her little finger
Caressing her eyebrows.

The door shut silently
When the rain had stopped. She was not
Wet. I said,
"What do you know of fury? What
Do you know of power? What do you know of anything
But the self-indulgent passive beauty
Of the rose? What do you know of an engine
Throbbing with joy and strength?
Of a broke-down engine, decayed and useless,
Of an engine without a driving wheel, helpless
To repair itself, unable to sprout
Or moan? What do you know of anything
But the unmoving sterile stillness of the rose
Who have sat in the rain and spread your fingers?
What can you know.... of anything
But roses!"

ALEX RAYBIN | 193

The Strength of Willows

To toy with living
And find ourselves a home
In a land where oak-leaves gibber
Is a hard thing, beloved.

The strength of willows is my gift
But can it allay the fury of those
Whose only home is madness
Where between the stars like smoke
From some abandoned lantern
The cosmic eight balls roll
Along the hairy table
Of our loss and fall?
          All
That glitters is not a golden girl
With apples in her hands. Your gift
Was less than mine and hardly
Yours to give seeing how much
A part of you it was. — An acceptance
Of weakness and sin without reproach, --
Love, — without conditions. It was
Enough.

      Together we can try to love
Our image of ourselves
                if not
Each other.

A Letter

It's not
Your ignorance I mind
Or that you think me
A hedonist insensitive
To how deeply you feel.

You are
A whirlpool-goddess
Everything comes near
Absorbed, churned,
And flung away
But you yourself
Unchanged, a continuum, metaphysical cunt
Cannot be trusted
Or quelled.

What draws me most
Is your loneliness the implacable
Placenta crying to be touched,
Penetrated, ripped away.
I want to shove
My prick into your heart.

If you loved me you would not know me
If you knew me you would not love me cannot love
                                        anything
More powerful than flesh:
Hate the bull
But fascinated by the horns.

Poem for Martha

The eight of swords, a woman
bound, hoodwinked, standing tiptoed
  on muddy ground, eight swords standing
  in the ground around her she feels bound
but she is free the swords do not
surround her cannot see a castle
      behind her her mouth clenched tight
      her hands grasping each other
          behind her back O lady
          of the swords O lady   lovely
              flying dragon in   the sky no one
              can or will step lightly O

ALEX RAYBIN | 195

Me to You

          my arm full of needles my
          heart full of holes and bones
bare and unadorned
                    without flesh or pretenses.
                                        My love
you have empty garments.
                              There is nothing in them
but you.

Dream

Naked angels sing lustful songs,
Playing on mahogany mandolins
In the holy dark of the last car
Of the D train; wending its cavernous way
Over bloodstained rails to the eldritch Bronx.

The first cars are filled
With the wails of weeping lovers
Crying for their longlost loves,
(All prostitutes now in a redbrick building
On Park and 34th, run by a two-headed pimp
With green buttonholes in place of eyes.)
And an old Negro crying for a pint of Scotch
He thinks he lost, but actually drank
Twelve years ago, on February 30.

The center cars are filled with empty air,
And an uninteresting white whale, quite dead by now,
Who tired of the nautical life.

I ride on top of the thirteenth car
Held by one glued-on finger
And one nailed-on toe.

"This subway is going to Cuba!" the loudspeaker
In the dark at the top of the tunnel
Announces. But can never reach Cuba,
Or Home.

Sunny Day

Seeing
the sky
come down
to greet me
I realize
it is an extension
of my self.

A huge black
      crow
flies overhead. This bird
is my totem

        In the beginnings
my ancestor,
Kilalumba,
        came down
from the sky
and sanctified this land
through ritual violence
and horrible human
self-sacrifice
to the three-headed dragon
he could not slay.

II
>   Or say
I
am the crow,
>   the sky
my father,
>   my ancestor
a trickster-mantis
the sacred dragon
has enclosed
>   in the oak
>   of the world
to escape someday
and violently regenerate
the primal chaos—

Nothing is changed.

My skin,
pale,
almost transparent
>   enough
to reveal my watery blood
is unaffected

My ritual amulet
will protect me from the plague
if it is not too late
already

I and my universe one
Unsophisticated
>   idea
sail together on our dark-prowed boat
toward the tributaries of Acheron. I think
I see my mother
(The third head of the dragon)
Smile as I pass her shaded figure.

JOEL SLOMAN

Power Failure

1

                    the reflection of a car on a window across
the street
no words come to my head.
The violence I'm afraid of is inside me.

The scene outside looks so static and unchangeable, except
    when someone walks by, who I can't hear—not the
    steps or the words.
Dust flies by, occasionally a pigeon. sky mostly flat gray,
    sound of plane,
bus, someone yelling.
Unspeakable confusion there is here.
I hate to write about some time other than the present. I
    shouldn't, though.
But I should talk about the past in its proper perspective.
Time is short. Yet we have all the (pigeon) time in the
    world.
clanking, banging downstairs
Sunday afternoon, I already talked to Michele and Jean on
    the phone.
Very cloudy. I'm thinking more of food than the poem.
I should read Poe for school. I know that someone around
    here could be very happy because of, not in spite of,
    the weather.
When a bus passes by, house shakes.

2

Is our patriarchal society becoming matriarchal?
Then it's a strange kind of matriarchy.
bronze Lachaise
nowhere on this continent such breasts as yours
Matriarchy, shit!
nothing's as simple as that   everything inside is closed

and so I learned my lesson, it's tough for women too.
　　cars don't bother to stop around here

This is what's going on inside me
pressure on my eyes

They're throwing us out of our offices and we're not even
　　prophets.
Or they're tripling the rent on account of ideas we sincerely
　　hold.
　　　　　　　　fingernails just long enough to tap on table

3
Here I indulge myself with bright lights, a romantic but
　　affected candle
and small Japanese holder that's red and cost a dollar, that
　　brightness,
source of all pleasure, to indulge oneself at all in times like
　　these, or
any time,
and he, upstairs, cries, screaming *I love you* in the midst of a
　　loud,
childish argument...then she cries, after throwing him out.
Noise is a problem. Roger Laporte screamed for water

God, protect us from this, this...what?

　　????????????

Tonight, a real power failure.

Poem

hold my breath as there's a sound on the stairs

foolish mind, mending and going mad at the same time　to
　　encounter once again the psychologist I once went to,
　　to offer proof of rehabilitation

I haven't been rehabilitated   garlic croutons in broth for a
    change

SAM. I don't know if my count is right, but I think twelve
    so far of the mobile missile launching sites destroyed.
    We only seem to lose planes to "conventional ground
    fire" meaning the peasant gets the credit.

moaning from the street, shrill television jazz from the next
    apartment.
my posture bad
disheveled bed
                        nights I haven't been able to
                        do anything
waiting for a phonecall

find out about Hell's Angels preparation for November 20th
    encounter with VDC
who dares to possess that style, a very muscular image,
    erotic
If I fear contact, I fear violence
I touched Stephanie's arm apologizing to her tonight   I'd
    love to dance

"In the backward countries (and perhaps not only in the
backward countries), the emergence of free societies depends
on fundamental social and economic changes which would
abolish existing inequality, privilege and repression.
Communism could carry through these changes (which are
the historical prerequisite, not the advent of liberation)."

nothing   I think, I believe   to be a naked animal

People hold me to systems of thought I don't believe, codes
    of behavior I don't live by   sometimes feel like
    intensification of average

Voices that fade, love that dies
I apprehend you, I no longer feel one way or the other
about you.
The air around the ineffable is intense.

cold creeping up from my legs to my bowels, stomach
moon, and not being able to say what one wants to say

blind pianist led by accordionist
"Now what?"

music swells

At Midnight

Getting blue lips from standing out there in the cold, I
twice
blew kisses that were never meant to be so open a gesture,
too near to
bleeding in public. Monuments soluble in revolutionary
fervor,
pleasant smoky orange embers, meat and fat burning,
wicked pin prick of time, prehistory, the conspiracy of
evolution,
steaming early forests, green and smoky impassable wall of
time
leading up to the five syllable line, or what we know of as
bleeding,
crop rotation, progress rationalization not innovation, and
yet all
those entrails sopped up by dusty tracts of land, slaughter
slowly,
the meat tastes better. We are going to look like filmy light
to
one another in the incorporeal period tomorrow, a recess
from bodies,
buildings and colored liquids.

The milk of human kindness
asserts itself, the people of tender ages find longing and all
passion unreal. Sensible union and flesh disappearing,
    philosophy
swallowed by its systems, poetry darning socks.
A plant of ecstasy and success. Creating endless spasms of
    words,
Goethe's glosses of the midnights of childhood, youth and
    maturity,
graves bearing flowers, boats glancing at the shore.
We are living in history, turn the pages deliberately, our
    names
are written in the water of government files, flee to the
    Caucasus
which separate a lake and a sea. It's so simple. I am
limited by the vast party of undone things, vile sensuous
    anticipation,
uncaught diseases and passions, unending night of internal
nervous life, imagination equally funny, dark night of the
dark night, tumbling between distant poles, stellar plastique.

Clay Pipe

The clay pipe smells and clinks
on the table like plaster of paris.
You come like the idle smoke and
your white thighs gleam
like a clay pipe. Japan in which
it was made is full of dark
lakes and dark green forests. To write
a short poem looking into someone
else's eyes! Energy, if you had a
bastard son, whose son would it be?
My eyes rest on you though
you're far away. Not clay, but
provocative movement where

the flesh feels so human. Why do
we need a rest or have no
hope of becoming official? I grip your
body and there is life, bricks and
drugs; a cure and a fatal device for resurrection.
There are two things without a single
meaning. I depend on you and color and
smell and taste and touch and hearing. Is
it idle or do I love you, my
sanity?

Blueprint

I keep thinking of isolated Long Island estates
with rolling lawns, swimming pools and the distant clinking
    of plates
on the verandah. The people, always seeming to warn
each other of the rules of behavior: how to eat corn
on the cob, how to walk, talk, drink, and deal
with the inconvenience of nature, the perfect meal
being a criticism of the accidental arrangement of the
    universe.
All solemnity in America is perverse,
all sophistication, a labyrinth that looks like a necessary
rationale. An identity a gleaming estate, isolated from class,
    the incendiary
vehicle that makes a true revolution possible. Experience is
    what we learn
from, not the fantasy of our self-programming, as if only a
    handful of experiences turn
out to be useful. All blueprints are specks in the
eye of history.

Love Song

Sex is a spiritual sojourn
in that land of tenderness/that cannot last
and we weep the lyrical irrelevance of our love.

* * *

Song is a land of spiritual loneliness
when the singer/like a bird/
awakes and sings
                    in heart of night
                                        (in some boughed tree.)

Yours is the land in which I awake and sing;
yours the rising heaventree:
to test out my soul against this dark embrace
requires strictest bravery

For beautiful and close in the dark as you are,
you are still a land of loneliness to me.

From *Paschal Poem:*
*Now in the green year's turning**

Part Three

(*Dream Dialogues*)

 Run, run, run with the rising moon!
The people are sleeping in calico,
and you (my heart) do not know where to go.

  The older poet said to me:
   Your poems have grown tough,
   but not tough enough.

 * This is the third part of a four-part poem.

Pity is like a river.
It walks like me,
though.
(How can I get away from my bones?)

The way rain pours into flat rock...
that kindly pity soaks into me.

Carpenter,
lay out smoothe nails/and
piece me together:
sand the rough planks,
but admire the smooth and fine-grained
of my soul.

                        (I thought that I
                            would never find
        song: a kinder wind
                            until I found
                                a wind gone blind.)

I know—
you will tell me
I am
...too gentle:
I cannot last:
I have had that feeling, too
                            (about you.)

(The wind—the world, shifted into
            a deeper color blue.)

Monseigneur:
        everything is wrong with me:
        for one thing: I have no...right
        to feel such a bone-tenderness
        for one of my same sex.

* * *

[*Finger-to-lip:*]
Creature is tired. Creature doth need rest.

* * *

Shoulders like ships, come over the corn
thrashing silence
and a kind of blue sky (sheaved, shelved),
—a slow spoken creature.

[*Very still:*]

               (Is my infirmity
               the reason why
               when people touch my body
               I feel shy?)

Wildflower opening to the wind—
O Lord! there is the word the lame
can speak only to you...
(why must I live out my life in this frame?)

I keep searching the word to transform
me
    ...into a renaissance boy again;
keep waiting, breathlessly, for some god
to lay his hand upon my shoulder, and
transform the bone into the wing.

Or some god, listening, to lay his hand
upon my body
and...whisper, it is enough/to be a poet...

---

and *this* may be the word of the mystical
         and this of the green, impossible
              longing
                 of
                    spring.

* * *

Beyond mere nakedness
stands something else:
a further reach I strain to bring to light:
and this I bore, I bared to him:
To dare to look the angel in the eyes.

I touch my body—and I leap toward God!
(I swear, I do not speak these words to shame:
 they labor forth through deep, inarticulate praise):
It is a joy beyond—beyond!
I offer this as proof of Him:
the ultimate embrace: the ecstasy.

(after the Japanese)

Through the haze of exhaustion
I gaze out at my friend
and am grateful for even the smallest mercy—
I am ecstatic
and could kiss his feet
and his shining face of an angel

and this exaggeration is, I know
...pitiful

(but earth's every mercy is measured by a mood.)

Archer

I keep seeing/landscapes
                    in the brain
(the gift's been driven in
                    that keen.)

I keep fearing/stars
        inside the skull
(the wound's
          that beautiful.)

I waken to the heartbeat
        in the vein
          that round
            the mind
              is wound

and hear the rushing in of rain
   into the soul's receiving ground.

* * *

With fire are the strict stars slain.

* * *

I tell you as the arrow's clean;
I tell you as the heart is plain,
so will the soul endure/hold green
     the shafts of song—
      the dark Orphic shine.

The shots are called,
I call the shots my own.

(for 'Poems of Two')

Again and again
we were able to stir up that wind
(over a cup of coffee)
that is friendship

—a kind wind
                    (that stirs over no other landscape or
                                              pastoral)
(vaguely erotic)
of warmth and longing
that goes beyond
                    (and would transcend)
the grace—and range
mere friendship lends.
            (After all,)
(the very dream of gods and angels is to bend.)

The Anemones of Collioure

I

Hooded anemones darken the Sunday morning February market,
tight crushed bunches, above crates of chickens and rabbits.
They are like hooded dark blood—purple and blue and red—
buried in the shouting orange of calendula and the chartreuse gestures of mimosa.
Behind the flower market hang beef carcasses,
grained in gristle and fat, red blood less a blood red
than that of the crowded flowers. The dark flowers seem full of spent passion, as if a god
had poured his passion into the flowers of a Sunday market.

II

Anemone drift below the rise and fall of tide-pool trash.
Below the cigarette carton—*Gauloises Bleu* thrust in and out through the rocks—
the rayed grey tentacles drift, or a greyed green dyed purple.
An orange peel drifting back and forth settles toward the tentacles and I feel
my finger retract as in the February water when I had felt
those tentacles explore for a softness of hand. The shore
is full of mouths, and all of them hungry. The hunger licks out from crevices in the rocks,
tastes and rejects the peel which something will not find trash.

III

Sometimes on anemone mornings when I walk by the eating sea,
I think of all the resurrections of the past, cut-down life flowering
into an ecstasy of color. I think of folded sepals opening out into a noon
gorgeous and trembling, of the fat pistil powdered with pollen
so purple as to be black, purple only as a stain on the hand,
and of the filaments' swollen anthers spilling black pollen on the stained
red sepals. For life riots, the dead wind flower
pressing into brightness in the still room above the restless sea.

IV

And then it endures death, a descent into slime.
If there is apotheosis, I must be its apotheosis, who see it in the rayed flower of the sea,
its colors muted into flesh, or who find it drifting
through memory, a smoky closed blossom over and over and over flaring toward life.
Yes, yes. In the dark tides of the sucking heart, a shape
opens and closes like a mouth. I listen
to the surge of its slip-slop syllables. The voice of the sea,
straining, shapes a word as if I were its name.

Rain Portrait

Materials: The tree. The summer lake, the river, the
winter lake.

Memory: I remember summer;
I remember trees and climbing,
a lithe summer wound with flutes and leaves.

The days: One day there was a river....
One day a boy and a girl danced.
One day there was a tree....(something about a
tree).

Memory: The greens of that year coil against summer's
heat.
Their green world waits, tangent to warped
light.
There are shouted voices, but their violence
dumb.

Detail: That god of the tree was green,
moving just out of reach, a patch of light
on the dark green and that green god moving,

arching against true sky
celebrations of blue and green
more certain than leaves....

Detail: The dance hall jutting out against 1939
crashes blare beer and whiskey
on neon sand.

Spangled night-whips lash a yellow floor.
Tablecloths, checked red on white, consume
a freight of elbows, fists, tight grins.

Oblique musicians snarl our summer on,
jostle, yellow on yellow crushed,
laughter, hard, on yellow window frames,

rub against our arms blunt dreams.
Black trumpets stammer red on the sawdust
floor.
The lake, an enveloping black, tugs at the shore.

Landscape: All worlds are unsatisfying, even dream's
defeated springs, false autumns, winters of
illusion snow.
I built a random summer out of home-made
gods....

Detail: The end of summer was a river night
suspended from unlikely shores.
Our shore was darker, smaller than the
glittering one.

"This is where you wanted to go?"
"I like the river at night."
"Have you been here long enough?"
"Yes."

Words, indirections in the dark,
a bobbing saraband of death:
mirrors wrestling stars.

Portrait: By the lake, three boys—seven, nine, fourteen—
fish from a little dock,
imperishable, intact.

But perishable, you, I know,
walk an improbable place, wound in false green,
where agile leaves assemble antic flesh.

Was there a god of the tree that put on flesh?
I have lost his green
in the green of a lake, grey rain, green trees.

The waters rise; the rain sways through the sky.
There is renewal in flute, in leaf;
but an elemental light—private, personal, pure—

moves, vanishes, where I have never been:
a climbing green, a rustle in the tree,
a shadow lost as rivers of night.

The lake is dappled with rain. The night moves
in.

Dolphin

I 6 a.m.

The net eases, swaying into the sea,
a drift of loose cords, mouths opening
into blue hunger. Its memory of hands
sinks through schools of desire. (*Not yet.*
Now. *Not yet.* Now.) Lead facts
tug, a taste of suspended hands
flicking beneath the hull. Flavor shapes
into the gauze funnel of a sigh.

II 9 a.m.

Gliding, he rides wave crests' clashing,
a torpedo summer crashing
porcelain lace, turns shoreward, driving.
They shatter to mercury splinters, flashing
under the black thrust of his snout, diving.

He circles the ghost shroud that guards them.
A flavor brushes his mouth. He is god, huge

in the shallows, baffled by ghost cords.
They shuttle in death harbor, gloved fears.
He puzzles a taste of wavering hands.

III   3 p.m.

How many hours prodding his goad snout into the yielding seine,
testing, circling a dream shroud, before its invitation mouth
flaps open to the black mouth driven in, the net
like a lace skin caught on his shoulders, sealing behind trapped tail?
A tussle of frenzy netted within the net, a roil
of thrashing darkness that charges the bright catch,
he becomes sea—starved, insatiable: mouth.
Teeth tear at fish, net, floats, though snarled cords weave pain.

IV   6 p.m., 7 p.m., 8 p.m.

Drowned, he hung in the bruised sea, his catch of nets
                    ripped like torn sleeves.
                              He is strange on the beach.
"He ate all of the fish. Then he ate at the nets."

Now he is netted by flies.
"He was so bad, we have a week mending."
                    Nets tore; floats tore loose in his dying.

In one stroke, an axe severs his tail.
"I never knew a fish like this one. My arms are sore from the dragging."
    When the head falls free,
a great tide of blood changes the sunlight.
    Four men drag the carcass to the truck.
"We sell him. He owes that much for the holes in the nets."
    Memory smears on the sea:
minnows flash in dark stains; something vanishes, as if dodging a question.
    The discarded tail and the worthless head
are not part of any dolphin now.
    The stiff tail, huge,
is an emblem on strange sand. (The nets have been dragged off, spread on rocks.)
"He was proud, that one, though."
The sun is already behind the mountains. The black head is dry.
    It is black suede.
            Its eyes
stare away from the deserted sea, away from the nets, the empty beach—
                        toward mountains,

Fish

1936–1940: Buffalo, New York

I

The greenhouse at Delaware Park moves me whenever I
        move through my lost rooms,
its pool of goldfish and golden carp silent beneath the palms.
Each spring the palms move out to decorate graduation
        halls. Then I dreamwalk up from the lake,
entering by a side door to meet the green darkness of an
        undecorated pool.
Its coat of algae still sifts into sooty eyes and furry walls,
though I know the building is down. I stare into the dark.
From a black pool flashing light, whispers of eyes loom.
From a darkness that is my last allegiance, silence calls me
        home.

II

We trade fish, or buy them from Mr. Trask, whose bathtub
        basement is awash with fish.
I see a cloudy face pressed against glass in pursuit of mollies
        and moons.
A school of zebras swims across eyes; a catfish questions a
        mouth.
From the dark, Mr. Trask, enormous, swims into view.
We buy baby moons—six for a dime—because they last and
        because they are cheap.
The pursuing net brushes hair. Vallisneria swirls in the
        turbid water.
Before you disappear, you lift a vague signalling hand. It is a
        shape.
It is full of snails and streaks of light and bright red flecks of
        live water.

1965: Collioure, France

I

Ah, with bright various light and with filters and love,
                              Monsieur Muller tends his fish.
Madame Muller serves us strawberry tarts and schnapps.
                    Every night with daughter and net,
Monsieur Muller visits tidepools in search of shrimp.
                              "Obsessed!" Madame Muller says,
but she smiles. In crystal, fish dance. The immaculate tank
                              compels us, who crowd the room.
A crystal dance is thrusting into spring a dozen filtered
                              smiles. In the crushed room
its sea-saw rhythm thrums. The place fills up with light.
                              From the window a whisper says,
"Yes" in a roll of pebbles. We are caught in a dance. The
                              dance is a net.
It drifts into brightness. Madame Muller smiles. "Obsessed!"
          she says. A bright commotion dances with the fish.

II

There are aquarium days that stretch the length of summer.
We row across them, bathed in sky.
Dolphin surface, islands that drift on summer
when horizons blur. Out of a haze of water,
like grey clouds, great fish sweep our sky,
a texture of light, immense above the bent water.

Statement

The elements of sight compose themselves—
sky-blue, grass-green, earth-brown—
into a landscape familiar and vague as breath.

The natural pattern flowers in its time.

But in another time the pattern holds
pollen on anther,
hawk wing spread against sky.

Gathering instants,
we move from time to time,
catching each other's images in streaks of light.

Transparent moments
chart black night's
calendula day.

I meet you in a sky of bursting flowers.

JOHN STEVENS WADE

Ticktacktoe

When I became myself I had
to say over and over, "give
your life to a straight line; cross
here and you lose, and if you stay
you gain."

        I didn't know once
what it meant to go forward.
So many lines were there to follow:
O's I made, and X's made
by others—not one connecting.

My infant son—it may have nothing
to do with this—my son reaches
and feels, where his legs meet, the line
he finds beyond his straight body.
He looks at me. He is fingering
the soft flesh. He doesn't know.

"Nobody"

I think of the blond child on the westward train.
Over and over on the midnight coach
the metronome of her words kept time with the rails.
"Nobody," she said over and over.
"Nobody." And when the lights of Topeka
flickered across her face in a bluish flame,
she leaned toward the swaying aisle of darkness,
and she said it vaguely, and finally
afraid, she pressed her body slowly back,
and said it so gently; so sweetly to the train
that carried her from one darkness into the next.

Upstairs

I went upstairs
to watch it move.
I kept it there
under some clothes
in a small box.
It felt so warm
when I held it.
Then I dropped it.
It didn't move
for a long time.
And the next day
when I touched it,
it felt funny.

It wouldn't crawl.
It wasn't warm.
Something was bad
inside. I knew
it wasn't mine
the way it was.
It's still up there.
I don't want it
because it's cold.
I won't go near.
I stay downstairs.
It's warm down here
and I'm happy.

The Goat Milkers

No no no no, they were too far apart;
they were too headstrong together.
And so I watched them when the living
came hard; they were much further out,
dying no doubt, alone in their house
after dark. And every morning,
coming down the valley for milk,
I'd always see one trailing the other.
They, too, were going to milk the goats,
and silently, file back to die
no doubt. No no, no waving or smiling,
just walking, one behind the other.
They were much further out than they thought:
always living together without talk,
almost touching but always apart.
No no no no.

Jigsaw

Good as gold, fine as
silk: two old cliches
remembered when the stoves
had nickel-plated fronts
and Model T's would kick
like mules. And I remember
days of silver after
the first snow; remember
the smell of chive, clove;
taste the checkerberry
on a sugared spoon.
It runs together: pail
after pail of water
down that timeless river.
The child discovers; the man
remembers. And nothing is lost.
Most of the gold and silk:
cliches of a childhood
that somehow fit together.
I'm still finding pieces.
I'm still picking them up.

Beyond the Panther

Beyond the panther back
of any morning there is
a land you've never seen
and a way to do the smallest
things and to live by them.
And in one place, one man
can follow the years that come
to him, and be content
with them. And then there is
the man who wants to ride

the panther. He doesn't stay
in one place, but he would
be the first to tell you where
the smallest things are hidden.

Jimmy's Father

When I was young
I would go over
to Jimmy's house.
I went again
years later and
I was busy
all afternoon
finding the street
where Jimmy lived.

Jimmy's father
opened the door
and shook my hand.
He hadn't changed.
He told me he
was Jimmy, and he
(Jimmy's father)
was dead. Had been
for years. For years!

He wasn't Jimmy.
Jimmy would know.
He wouldn't sit
and lie about
the things we did;
about the things
I knew we didn't
and couldn't do.
Jimmy's father
wouldn't tell me
where Jimmy lived.
He kept talking
about himself.

The Ascent

I tell you man must
burn his fingers—touch
the sun. He must drill his
eyes with stars. And when he
cracks open, the woman comes.
She will wrap the bandage.

The salve of her hands will ease
his mind. He'll think: "Man is
everywhere—at the woman's
thigh, on the nipple's top."
And he'll dream-dream-dream
from the darkest pit. He won't
look down. He can't. The plant
of his spine shoots up-up.
all the way. At the top
he won't stop thinking of planets
and stars. He'll still feel her
hands salving the sores.
And there's always the going up
to make him dizzy, almost
crazy. And he loves it.

Body Job

They tore me down and flushed
my insides. Keeping
my eyes, I watched them steal
my legs. When one of them
cut himself, I stood
helplessly on my bones,
pretending to be dumb.
In my skull I kept
a memory of legs.
My thoughts were scattered
before me like keys,
and they walked on them
trying to open me.
All afternoon I felt them pulling,
pushing, holding me up.
Their hard hands fingered
the tissue of old wounds.
At dusk by the window

my chest was taken.
The cut moon rose
in the patched sky. It was then
I saw the soaked parts
humped like islands
on the floor. In the moonlight
they looked deserted without me.
Even then I wanted
to be whole in pieces.

Each to His Own Ground

In the high country people
aren't casual about the ground.
They notice grass, stumps,
worms. So many times
I've seen these people reaching
down as if to hold on.
But the peat-bog people
eye the trees. Remember
storms. For them the birds
and stars get turned around—
the peat-bog people think
this true, but they won't tell
me how they know. And high
in the country where people
are rooting, holding on,
such thinking is a hoax.
Each to his own ground.

NANCY WILLARD

In Brittany

They carry their lean bread
  like a wand, their water
from wells in the first light.
  The carrying will cure you,
they say. A miracle is being
  in the right place at the right
time, as local a matter
  as lightning, or the death
of a hen, or the sighting
  of a new saint.

You shall know him by
  his marvellous granite boat,
by his power to bring
  wolves to their knees, husbands
to hapless girls,
  and the swift rain.
He is rough as your Sunday coat,
  as warm and freckled
as a thrush's egg. What sign
  would you have?

The bagpipes whine in the wheat,
  the coiffed women advance,
like a protest of poplars, a sheaf
  of banners tasselling their hands.
In the saint's cave, a meadow of candles
  blows, and out of the common sleep
of first signs, a general dance
  begins: slow sickle, orchard shaking
with birds, dew lighting the field
  of a second waking.

O friends, it is very hard on the heart.
For your delight I devour loaf after loaf
of stale bread, till the silken tents sink to rest
and wide-eyed children, bogeyed to bed,
remember my cavernous mouth with fear.

Sometimes I pick at my food like a child.
The taste of the wire in the apple hurts.

I Knew a Boy Who Ran
with the Dogs

I knew a boy who ran with the dogs,
their muzzled heads rising and falling
like foam at a swimmer's neck,
or steeds past dragonflies
thin as barometer's blood.

Found by authorities, hidden
in a cellar like an antique saint,
accompanied by several companions
he tried to explain

how things were different at night,
how the shops with no people, seen
in the light of a dog's eyes,
shine like coral from an ancient sea

and a child in the park can't tell
people from statues
except, in a few, by the smell
and the eyes,

and how important it is to run
to keep alive, and not to belong
but to be, to run from the clocks and the kettles,

The Freak Show

I am Giuletta, the bird woman. I married
the rain man and learned to fly.
Together we walked the high wire
over trees, churches, bridges, green fields,
straight into heaven. We saw the white seed
after a child blows it, and were much praised.
Though I had nothing but him, I craved no more.

Even in falling he blazed like a star.
The next night I went on, knowing I could not fall.
A brave girl, the clowns told me. Then I cried.
I knew that people who never fall forget
danger is all and their blood goes dumb.
Listen, the ring-man said to me one night,
You've lost your shape. You've got no grace.
You're old.

Waiting in the dark trucks I am content to watch,
to nibble the sweet fruits that the dwarf brings.
We walk among the orchards and hear
the silence of tensed feet on the blessed wire.
So much walking affects the appetite, Madam,
says the dwarf with a sucking leer.
And so much sorrow gives enormous hunger.

I am round and simple as a Persian plum,
so earth-shaped now no wire could hold me
or support the weight of my fallow grief.
When you hear the dwarf crying the measure
of my marvellous flesh, you will crowd in.
Blinded by footlights, I hear you wallow
and whisper in the pit below my chair.

My God! Arms like tree trunks, cries a man's voice.
Must be hard on the heart, a woman blurts.

NANCY WILLARD | 229

the beds and square meals
to the round spinning world, where
only the dust settles.

The Church

If the walls are whitewashed clean, I hope
that under the show of purity I can find
a mural of monkeys pressing wine,
that below the candles on the choir stall

someone has carved a dancing bear or a boy
riding a wild boar.
The man who makes the dragon under the
saint's feet must know the dragon is

beautiful. And therefore, on the altar,
the Bible will rest on the back of a griffin
to remind you that the beast is present
in every birth.

You shall not exclude them from the communion
of saints and men. If the roof is plain
put a cock on the steeple; you shall not
exclude them from your marriages.

Wedding Song

Orpheus calling. The grass parts, the seas
lie down for Orpheus, the one
calling, without harp or hymn,
with his favored flesh, running
white as a summer's day.

warmer than grass and stone
    where the sun lay.
        Everyone running, running before
            Orpheus, who loses again
                and again, himself, calling.

The grove beats with voices, sees
    a wedding walking, trees
        harping and crying, Eurydike
            runs in a white dress, her train
                catching the burrs and the leaves falling.

We, strangers on a bridge, look down.
    The moss-wedded water shows
        a wedding walking through water cress
            and wild flags, turning; flows
                into the muddy bed.

Procession in weedy dress
    spins us around too late. For us
        the air burns with their having
            been, like a swing rocking
                where the child has fled.

The serpent that gnaws
    at love lies sunning
        in the song. Orpheus calling.
            Through the woods they pass,
                hand in hand, running.

the Word calling, the grass
    parts and the sea lies down
        before the hymn, himself, before
            this man who loves, who was
                before sea, grass, and all falling.

Crewel

"... all day she wrought with her Nydill, and that the
diversitye of the colours made the Work seem lesse tedious,
and contynued so long at it til veray Payn made hir to
give over."

(OF MARY QUEEN OF SCOTS)

In the crewel world of my grandmother
   a leopard bares satin teeth,
its jaws open less for hunting
   than singing. Trees round as puddings
fan into fruit where a monster
   parrot hangs like an earring in starstitch

and whipped spider's web. Nothing
   is born but seems to remember
itself on the void, meeting its own gaze
   on the simple water. The first idea lies
in the mind of the old woman

who has never seen peacocks or panthers
   but knows they wear mauve throats of crushed
iris and Gobelin, gold couching the wings.
   The squirrel or boar, sown
on the field azure of a minor kingdom

pushes up under the hand:
   herringbone for a hummingbird
wing, filoselle and crowsfoot
   for the flounced hills, knotted
cross furring the red deer that floats
   to a blue pagoda sunk in strawberries

where the tree of life hardly feels
   the fernstitch poppinjay twice its size.
Oaks and elephants such as Isaiah
   saw or Saint Brendan set
sail for and thought he arrived:

NANCY WILLARD | 233

the way the world strikes the eye
   of a man nearly taken out of it,
or an old woman half blind
   from so many buff hens and wild grapes
and thyme blooming at her hands,

bringing forth such sheep, such cocks
   in diamondstitch and shell, to march
forever round the brass bed, a woman
   praising in lovestitch with thread
all honey and indigo, a promise
   of lion and lamb and herself wed.

First Lesson

So I studied the egg, and everything I learned came from
that study
CONSTANTIN BRANCUSI

Holding this egg,
   detail
of Quaker plainness,
   familiar
as thee and thou,
   I hold the color and shape
of peace,
   whether blown and dyed,
balloon promising flight
   that a finger crunkles,
or boxed, the lid raised to show
   a jury noncommittal
as the bald heads of
   a dozen uncles.

The shape of peace
   is the certainty
of the simple thing:

as when a man draws
one line, known
    from the first
and it opens what we forgot.
    Unicorn understood
from the magnificent horn,
    so I know flight
without wings
    when a candle
against the shell shows
    only a milky light.

"Learn from the egg
    and the bird's wing,"
observed Brancusi, flapping
    about his room in red
sandals, his garden of
    sculpted birds spinning
on pedestals like patient
    and sleepy bears.
Tortoise of turquoise,
    birds waking in brass
and silver, harp
    that leaps from the bowels
of Orpheus
    says,

I am a harp raised
    to the first joy of my master's mind,
falling into myself like water
    and sleeping child.
Make birds, wings, planets,
    minerals, faces; nothing you gather
will sing so clearly
    how we are alive, nothing praise

the flight of a bird
   so well as this
round possibility,
   silence unshattered, temple soon
to be raised, the
   ancient word.

KEITH WILSON

bloodtotem

the pig mask upon the wall
has carved eyes & a snout
ridged & grooved by knife

the pig mask upon the wall
has four eyes: two for it,
two for a man in looking through

to see the world in a charge,
grasses flashing by, in red eyes
inflamed to a boar's hatred

the pig mask upon the wall
is its own incantation, unleashes
tusked furies, old fears

of lunging, driving lusts
—blood & fighting, ripped
bellies, clicking teeth

& the sweet warmth of blood
trickling down the jowls: pig
mask, upon the wall. passive.

in tension. made of man the mask
startles the breathing, holds
in ceremonial wood the imaged

ancient king, killmaster
of the ages: with a warrior's cry
he bears the mask before him

a lens of gleaming wood
while out of darkness behind
comes a snuffling, & luminous eyes.

The Horses
(*two paintings by Hsu Pei-hung*)

It's the way I conceive myself sometimes:
hammerheaded, bigfooted, but running loose
in black meadows.

>   Just at dusk,
> the rice paper crashing beneath my hooves
> every muscle a brushstroke, heavy with pigment, I,

>   alive with the race
>   of line, up, out.

ii

Or his five horses, standing in a field
looking over far gates or running hard & black
off shining paper:

>   all five are real enough
> to ride, mine, a blaze on his forehead, slashes
> the turf with his black hooves, neighs, and
> thunders into my livingroom, shitting on the floor.
> Damned horses that break a man's home up!

The Streets of San Miguel

What have I to bring them, in their
stillness?

>   dark youths, lounging
> by the one public phone, old ladies
> headed for Mass, the soft wind
> against their dark dresses.

                              If I lived here all my life,
spoke Spanish as fluently as I dream I do,
if one of these lovely boys loved one
of my lovely girls & I was elected mayor,
still I'd be a broken Anglo poet
who has, I'm told, strange eyes,
stranger ways—

             who must turn
everything to words while they, so alive
need so few to speak their loves.

The dusty street, quiet in moonlight,
stretches out ahead. I take a strange walk,
going nowhere. I have nowhere to go.
The ancient houses ring a pathway
to high, windswept mesas.

The Gift

—for Kathy

this is a song
about the gift of patience

of opening

the need to walk alone
ever, deeper, into

this is a poem
against light

a recommendation
to darkness

bring a candle
the room is warm

this is a song

Old Love

Coming down

       I, on

   Bright Angel

trail, below Kaibab, the long
turning into history and back
towards rock: I suddenly see you,
gone all these years, inset
a fossil leaf, trapped before time,
it is an echo of yourself that sings
the sad notes, these dry notes. Sweet
Gone Canary, turned to dust puffs
caught by the wind racing across blue
canyons, wherever you are, gone blue
and rose, against sandstone or falling
neon across the low clouds, too large
a part of me gets lost in this coming down.

the singer

(*from* "Graves Registry")

who did sing, whose voice
spoke out of a guitar's darkness;
in a clear young night he
sang midwatches away, telling

of country lands, of growing crops
green corn, tall in the fields
of Kentucky; dark songs of loves,
concerns and ancient questions
he had not yet lived to confirm
or deny.

17. About 6′1″. Heavyset,
with plowman's hands & walk.

Then there was my gun.
In its way, it sang too. Clean machine
oiled & perfect, the slide flashed
back over my relaxed hand pow. pow. pow.
& .45 wadcutter slugs crimped neat holes
in the fluttering paper; the gun
was a happiness to my hand.

Many nights that boy was the whole
watch as I would lean against the flying
bridge, coffee growing cold in my cup,
listening to that voice singing out
the darkness ahead.

Then came the time in port. Just before
the invasion. The gunners mates were
cleaning all weapons for the coming action &
claimed mine too.

I was on the bridge
checking the charts. An indistinct
popping sound. Silence.
Running feet, & shouts.

When I got back to the fantail
he was lying there, his boy's face
twisted & grey, big farmer's hands
held in his guts, guitar beside him.

My gun in the destroyed mate's hand.
Smoking faintly.
These are the things get lost.
Guitars. Guns. Hands to hold
onto them.

The Hanging of Billy Budd

the quick

—jerk.

I

what would a man
see if his eyes
were not blindfold?

the stretching sea?

a wake bubbling
blue, behind the gulls
a darkness?

a young face
halfshut eyes
looking out

what would they
see?

II

an innocence

    (no thing
stands as innocent as the

sea, knowing no
　　wrongs, a simple
　　　　power

in one man
the flash of a knife
awakens, dark thunders

all men perhaps facing the
same in this fierce
excitement
and at a man's
own death?

rough tickle
about the neck, wind
kicking at the hair
high above, looking
down

what would he see
but the easy pitching
ship, the pale faces
the watch, assembled
below

an innocent sea
calm as God's eyes.

a poem for fathers
—for R.C.

facing the uncertain stillnesses
within them, their own ages
what they come to
barriers

a small blonde girl
stands, has blue
eyes, thin oval face

& what she asks
what she
demands

is the singing
we have guarded
all these years

JAY WRIGHT

The End of an Ethnic Dream

Cigarettes in my mouth
to puncture blisters in my brain.
My bass a fine piece of furniture.
My fingers soft, too soft to rattle
rafters in second-rate halls.
The harmonies I could never learn
stick in Ayler's screams.
An African chant chokes us. My image shot.

If you look off over the Hudson,
the dark cooperatives spit at the dinghies
floating up the night.
              A young boy pisses
on lovers rolling against each other
under a trackless el.
           This could have been my town,
with light strings that could stand a tempo.
        Now,
          it's the end
          of an ethnic dream.
I've grown intellectual,
go on accumulating furniture and books,
damning literature, writing "for myself,"
calculating the possibilities that someone
will love me, or sleep with me.
Eighteen-year-old girls come back from the Southern
leers and make me cry.
              Here, there are
              coffee shops, bars,
              natural tonsorial parlors,
              plays, streets,
              pamphlets, days, sun,
              heat, love, anger,
              politics, days, and sun.

Here, we shoot off
every day to new horizons,
coffee shops, bars,
natural tonsorial parlors,
plays, streets,
pamphlets, days, sun,
heat, love, anger,
politics, days, and sun.
        It is the end of an ethnic dream.
        My bass a fine piece of furniture.
        My brain blistered.

On the Block: Another Night Search

I

"Block time, baby, let's walk."
And we walk to our extension
in the Harlem night, going nowhere,
watching the legs challenge the blasé evening.
Any light and laughter
and bass-endowed jukebox can pull us.

II

I've come this way alone.
I've jutted up in bars with winding mirrors,
for a quick beer, a quick glance
at some unapproachable liaison,
where the ritual was so complete,
the code so unshakable that
everyone was his own intermediary.
I've seen the vulgar priests
scratch their hips to the archaic dances,
offer their eyes as tacit redemption.
No, it isn't the night we own,
but a way of seeing each other
when all the silly shops have caged their wares.

III

"You know it's the season.
Ain't nothin' to do but do it.
Here we are at the place to play,
if you can't get it here, it don't exist."
But it does. A go go
in a cameo face and a chilled motion,
envious of the leisure of eyes,
ambitious in the haunting expectancy
of an Orpheus with a muted lute,
horrible in the gregariousness of her thighs.
"And naw, welcome to the stage..."
A Billy Budd of a boy,
a hoarse didact of our liberal ways,
teasing to be choked by Queens matrons
who won't when he will
and will when he tosses
in his road-bound bed.

IV

A lonely man here, with the palpable
conciliators under every overcoat,
with the whisper of money under every tongue,
is a man undiscovered.
                        And we must walk again.
Not down that way, stretching like a banquet table
with gorged men nodding in their desserts.
Not that way, where shadows risk no identity.
Not that way, where ladies invite you
to apolitical, economic conferences.
Not that way, where psychic leave-takers
rake your mind for the seeds of your discontent.
Not that way, where brown bedraggled
doormen sniff at your existence.
Not that way, where cars tilt the board

of a highway that leads nowhere.
Where then?
Where?

V

But we are moving,
ignoring the eyes that sense
our truncated hilarity.
Stop? Not now.
Not even for the syndicalist
preachers whose beds are a passion,
whose feet are forever hooked
to the ceremonial ladders
of a monetary dignity.

VI

The lights run like Christmas cherries,
flung by a desperate mother
through the trees arching Seventh Avenue.
The hum of evening is like
the misguided twitting of mynah birds.
"I feel like dealin'."
But give no thought to this.
It is the culmination of the quest.
We have made it again.
We have come home from a place
we've defined with our presence.
Ah, sweet melodies.
Sweet world that is bought
with an anchored soul.
And I have searched them all
to find the running safe
where the subtleties are my own.
A possibility, a limitation.
A limited possibility.

The imagination of the daring
who see this black world whole.
"Get to that," he says.

VII

And naw, some home cooking.
The pots are on 'cause it's
any night you make it.
And downtown when you want it.
You've got to get next to something
and hold it 'cause it's a crying world.
Hey, now, president, here's your thing.
Smile. It's a dance.
And he again.
"It didn't build Chartres,
but it made me.
It's home, baby.
Finally, home.
Now, I think I can travel."

Death as History

i

They are all dying,
all the ones who make
living worth the price,
and there is hardly time
to lament the passing
of their historical necessity.
Young poets sit in their rooms
like perverted Penelopes,
unraveling everything,
kicking the threads
into the wind,

and I stop,
woolly-eyed,
trying to record
this peculiar American game.
But they are dying,
the living ones,
and I am sapped of all resolve,
fleeced, finally, of the skill
to live among these others.

To be charged with so much living
is such an improbability,
to be improbable about living
is such a charge to hold
against oneself,
against those who are dying.

ii

Dropping his history books,
a young man, lined against the horizon
like an exclamation point with nothing to assert,
stumbles into the dance.
The dancers go round and round
like drones on an unhappy flight.
They look to him for another possibility.
They hum.
They plead.
They circle him with outstretched hands.
They offer him their own salvation.
And he moves forward with a rose.
All that long search
to bring back death.
Who wants that old mystery?

iii

But still there is the probable.
And even in Madrid
the golden ages settle
in their sturdy coffins.
Oh, you can say that there
where the olive trees burst up
through the asphalt cells,
where well-endowed bulls butt
the tail-end of tame Sundays,
and the coquettish river flings
its hips at the cattle-mouthed mountains,
everything there is an imitation.
The girls always advance on the square,
repeating the vital moments,
needing no bookish priests
to redeem that dance.
And it is always the credible dance.

iv

It is always like the beginning.
It is always having the egg
and seven circles,
always casting about in the wind
on that particular spot;
it is that African myth
we use to challenge death.
What we learn is that
death is not complete in itself,
only the final going from self to self.

v

And death is the reason
to begin again, without letting go.
And who can lament

such historical necessity?
If they are all dying,
the living ones,
they charge us with the improbable.

The Sense of Comedy: I

Imagine yourself,
in the suit of lights,
strolling toward the barrier
as if you, alone, knew
the purpose of your coming.
You are suddenly erect,
suddenly the keeper
of a deeper knowledge.
You are suddenly another,
and yet yourself,
suddenly in control
of your own fear.
Right on time
without a sense of time,
you extend your hand
to become less private.
You turn to the stillness
of all these old
identifications.
Everything must be won again.
A clear call.
And the comedy begins, again.

AUTOBIOGRAPHICAL NOTES

JACK ANDERSON
'Jack Anderson was born June 15, 1935, in Milwaukee, Wis. He
has a B.S. in theatre from Northwestern University and an M.A. in
English from Indiana University. He has, at various times, been a pup-
peteer, a teaching assistant at the University of California (Berkeley), a
delivery truck driver, an actor with theatre groups in San Francisco, and
assistant drama critic of the Oakland *Tribune*. He is presently news editor
of *Dance Magazine*. His poetry has appeared in a number of magazines. He
has also written on dance for *Ballet Today*, *Ballet Review*, *Ramparts*, and the
Northwestern University *Tri-Quarterly*.'

  The Hurricane Lamp. Trumansburg, N.Y.: NEW/BOOKS, 1968.

G BISHOP-DUBJINSKY
'g bishop-dubjinsky was born on october 8th (the day of the heroic
guerrilla) 1946 at 11:23 pm'

BESMILR BRIGHAM
'Studied at New School for Social Research under Sidney Alexander, Mr.
Horace Gregory, Charles I. Glicksberg. . . . Since 1949 revolving back
and forth—Mexico, Central America, camping out, little chostas interior
villages. Involved in words. I wrote. Stuck papers into trunks, boxes.
Until Meg Randall made me see (feel), she and Sergio, that writing was
"reaching"—and not *for*. Three levels: moving time (present–past);
retention (the mind); an outward commitment to one's place, to another.
. . . An intensity of feeling due two writers: Mr. John Gould Fletcher and
Robert Duncan; each at such a distance in time . . . read—listened. And
to individual "little" editors who used from what I sent. Married. We
(Roy and I) raised a beautiful girl on the road.'

VICTOR CONTOSKI
'I was born in Minneapolis in 1936, obtained my B.A. (in classics) from
the University of Minnesota in 1959 and my M.A. (in English) in 1961.
The next three years I spent in Poland studying Polish and teaching
American literature at the University of Łódź. Currently I am: 1. married
to a beautiful woman; 2. working toward my doctorate at the University
of Wisconsin; 3. translating several exciting modern Polish poets.'

  Translator, *Four Contemporary Polish Poets*. Madison, Wisconsin:
    Quixote, 1967.

GAIL DUSENBERY
'Gail Sherrell Dusenbery was born in Albany, New York, in 1939 and
attended Cornell University and the University of California, Berkeley.'

  The Mark. Berkeley, California: Oyez Press, 1967.

DAVE ETTER

'Born March 18, 1928, Huntington Park, California
Has lived and worked at odd jobs in California, Kentucky, Iowa, Massachusetts, Indiana, and Illinois
Graduated from University of Iowa, BA History 1953
Presently working for Encyclopaedia Britannica as a writer
Married; two children
Has contributed over 200 poems to over 60 literary magazines and anthologies
Won two awards for first book of poems, *Go Read the River*: The Midland, Poetry Award and the Poetry Prize of Friends of Literature, 1967
Awarded a Bread Loaf Writers' Conference Fellowship in 1967
Currently completing a second volume of poetry, to be published in 1969.'

> *Go Read the River*. Lincoln, Nebraska: University of Nebraska Press, 1966.

GENE FOWLER

'Born October 5, 1931, Oakland, California. Didn't learn of need for glasses until age 8. Then learned of *dual* visual universes. Later generalized the concept. Tumor on chest early teens: two years thinking i was hermaphrodite. . . . Night club comic and mimic late teens. Developed 100 identities one as real as another. 3 years jungle and Army. 1 year armed robber. 5 years San Quentin Prison. 1 year stat work and computers (big 'uns). 5 years, so far, as poet. . . .'

> *Field Studies*. El Cerrito, California: dustbooks, 1965.
> *Shaman Songs*. El Cerrito, California: dustbooks, 1967.

DAN GEORGAKAS

Born 1938

'Consumer society decrees that art is a special category made by special men. Even the lives of the poets are stored as merchandise and marketed as part of the Spectacle. Lost is the sanity of the American Indian where the Word as Song was inseparable from life. Love songs were meant to win a woman and war songs to help one in battle. Every man was a poet who recognized the sky was his father and the earth his mother and all living creatures their children.'

> *Red Shadows* (prose). New York: RAI Corporation, 1967.

JOHN GILL

'I was born (1924) and raised in Chicago's South Side; Jackson Park and the Midway (lands set aside from the World's Columbian Expedition of 1893) were my stamping ground. Now, I live in the Finger Lakes region of New York alongside Taughannock Falls—the highest falls east of the Rockies.

Although I claim to be transient and dream of travel, I've lived upstate twelve years and keep accumulating more dogs, more cats, more barnyard pets to insure my continued rustication. I edit and print *NEW*: *American & Canadian Poetry* magazine and NEW/BOOKS.'

Young Man's Letter. Trumansburg, N.Y.: NEW/BOOKS, 1967.

JOHN HAINES

'Born June 29, 1924, in Norfolk, Virginia, the son of a Navy officer. Attended schools throughout continental U.S. and Hawaiian Islands. Served in the Navy during the Pacific War, 1943–46. Studied Painting and Sculpture in Washington, D.C., and New York at intervals between 1946 and 1951. First came to Alaska in 1947, and began writing poetry that same year. Since 1954 have been living at present address. I had a Guggenheim Fellowship for 1965–66, and this spring [1967] I went on a reading tour which took me to Michigan, Ohio, Wisconsin, New York, and San Francisco. Present plans include the possibility of more travel in the "Lower 48".'

Winter News. Middletown, Conn.: Wesleyan University Press, 1966.

PHYLLIS HARRIS

'Born Phyllis Masek, September 18, 1940, Gering, Nebraska. Small town big family   barefoot on ditchbank   dreaming of Indians.

'B.A. Loretto Heights College 1962. Junior year in Vienna, stehplatz, study. Bummed around Europe. Cave in Tenerife. Denver. Mexico. Boston. The Bowery. Took up with the Catholic Worker movement, soup kitchen, migrant labor. Sold newspapers to pay rent, peddled balloons.

'M.A. San Francisco State College 1964. Married Peter Harris. Daughter Cassandra born 1965 while her papa in jail for draft refusal. Now living in Catholic anarchist community.'

JIM HARRISON

'I am twenty-nine, married, and have one child. I was born and raised in northern Michigan where I would return if there were any way to make a living there.'

Plain Song. New York: W. W. Norton & Co., 1965

ROBERT HERSHON

'I was born in Brooklyn on May 28, 1936. Graduated from New York University. Worked for *Herald Tribune*, other newspapers and magazines since. Began writing poetry in San Francisco in 1961. My wife, Michaeleen, and I have two children.'

Swans Loving Bears Burning The Melting Deer. Trumansburg, N.Y.: NEW/BOOKS, 1967.

WILLIAM M. HOFFMAN

'Born New York City, 1939. Poet—poems published in magazines, set to music, and read in public. Playwright—Caffe Cino, LaMaMa (*Thank You,*

Miss Victoria, Spring Play, among others). Editor of *New American Plays* (Volume 2, published; Volume 3, forthcoming). Has worked in printing, book publishing. Presently on fire.'

EMMETT JARRETT
'Emmett Jarrett was born (1939) and raised in Louisiana, studied at Florida State until expelled in 1958, served in the Army and has lived in Chicago, New York, Paris, Greece. Last year he taught English in Crete. He and his wife Ann, who met in Babette Deutsch's modern poetry course at Columbia in 1963, now live in New York. He has been involved with two literary magazines: *things* (1963–65) and *Hanging Loose,* which still is.'

> *The Days.* Cambridge: Bean Bag Press, 1968.

SISTER MARY NORBERT KÖRTE
'Sister Mary Norbert Körte, O.P., is a San Francisco poet, teacher, musician, and member of the Dominican Order in the Roman Catholic Church. She is active in her Order's life of prayer, study, and the giving of the fruits of that prayer and study. Of her life, she says: "I must call myself a poet-religious-poet for I cannot separate the one from the other. To say that the religious life nourishes my poetry is to imply also the reverse. My poems are the voices of a relationship with God that exists within the framework of an Order dedicated to the freely joyous pursuit of Truth, Beauty, and Goodness." To say and be this is enough reason.'

> *Hymn to the Gentle Sun.* Berkeley, California: Oyez Press, 1967.

ROBERT LAX
'Robert Lax was born in Olean, New York, November 30, 1915. He is Roving Editor of *Jubilee* & editor and publisher of *Pax,* a one-page poetry magazine. He has been living in Greece for the past 6 years, mostly on the island of Kalymnos, & devoting himself entirely to poetry. His verse-play, *Drama,* was produced in 1967 by the BBC Third Program. *The Circus of the Sun* (in Spanish translation of Ernesto Cardenal) has appeared in several anthologies in Spain & South America.'

> *The Circus of the Sun.* Brooklyn, N.Y.: Journeyman Books, 1960.
> *new poems.* Brooklyn, N.Y.: Journeyman Books, 1962.
> *Thought.* Brooklyn, N.Y.: Journeyman Books, 1966.
> *3 or 4 Poems about the Sea.* Brooklyn, N.Y.: Journeyman Books, 1966.
> *Sea Poem.* Scotland: Wild Hawthorn Press, 1966.

ETHEL LIVINGSTON
'born june 7, 1947, in savannah, georgia. i have lived there all my life and attended schools virginia and new york. during the summer of '65, i spent two months at a writing school in aspen, colorado—and studied last year with denise levertov in a school workshop. at present, i am a junior at vassar college and am studying this year with david ignatow.'

DICK LOURIE

'Born December thirty-first   nineteen thirty seven in Hackensack New Jersey
raised in green metropolitan suburbs
and sent to school till I was twenty-two.
Teaching college freshmen to write essays
drove me to Europe to write and play jazz
and sing old American songs. Came back
and tried offices till age twenty-nine.
then started singing children's songs to make
a living / as I write thats where I am.'

   The Dream Telephone. Trumansburg, N.Y.: NEW BOOKS, 1968.

CLIVE MATSON

'California sagebrush wilderness my old haunt with
rabbits and coyotes, my favorite animal after
Goofy the Hound, I remember dawn sunbursts and the
orange glow layers under falling night,
from there to here in 26 years: I was born in
Los Angeles in 1941. Peyote in 1960 on, Huncke,
Andy Heath who my love will never fail for just now.
In New York today hanging together watching
the mind theater and listening to truth tapes
that reel in every brain. My hobbies: staying alive,
high speed laser photography can freeze those blurring
spirits that twist heads around, making love, dodging brain police,
casting lines into the near chaos from
magic frames.'

   mainline to the heart. Kerhonkson, N.Y.: Poets Press, 1966.

JASON MILLER

'Born in Hartford, Conn. Attended University of Connecticut. Army
hitch in Japan. Years of playwriting, travels around the country. Early
Hart Crane-Lorca-French school—influenced poems not making it.
Work at all sorts of jobs, mostly by choice, often seasonal: warehouse,
stock, post office, waiter, bartender, strawberry picking, clerk, guard,
"Manpower," etc. Play produced at Dallas Theater Center, 1961. A kind
of break-through in poetry with discovery of Williams and returns to
Rilke. Now living in Great Lakes area.

   'I believe, for some moments, a paradise possible on earth—even in
America—now.'

   Stone Step. Brooklyn, N.Y.: Jadis/Yumi Editions, 1968.

DOUG PALMER

'Born: April 21, 1941. Raised in the Sierra foothills, near Colfax, California. Made me pretty much a loner—by long experience. . . .

'I am working toward making my living as a poet. As part of this I write poems to people on the streets in San Francisco and at the University of California campus, Berkeley. I wear a sign saying that I will write poems for what people can give in return. I go by the name FACINO when I street write.'

> *The Quick and the Quiet.* Berkeley: Synapse Press, 1965.
> *Poems to the People.* Berkeley: Peace & Gladness Co-op Press, 1965.
> *Poems Read in the Spirit of Peace & Gladness.* Edited by Doug Palmer
>   and Tove Neville. Berkeley: Peace & Gladness Co-op Press,
>   1966.
> *Margaret's Experiences.* Berkeley: OR Press, 1967.
> *Basta.* Oakland: Doug Palmer, 4154 Piedmont Ave., 1967.
> *Moon Services.* Oakland: Doug Palmer, 4154 Piedmont Ave., 1967.

MARGE PIERCY

'I was born in a Detroit neighborhood closed like a boxcar, blocks black or white in paranoiac checkerboard near the Detroit Terminal Railroad and Lincoln Mercury plant. I was the first person in my family to go to a university, and it took me five years to recover from my education. I am now working on a novel about urban renewal in Chicago. I am a member of Students for a Democratic Society. I helped start an adult chapter in Brooklyn.'

> *Breaking Camp.* Middletown, Conn.: Wesleyan University Press,
>   1968.

ALEX RAYBIN

'Born December 6, 1945, in Florence, Italy. Li·ved in Rome to age 5, Lower East Side, Bronx slum, Bronx middle class neighborhood— High School of Science. North Carolina to college at Duke at 16, year and a half there, year in New York at CCNY and New School, another half year at Duke, left college, East Side, North Carolina, San Francisco, Berkeley, East Side, North Carolina, Berkeley, San Francisco, East Side since then, mainly writing, balling, taking drugs, travelling, surviving. One job as press agent for a film company, presently operating a coffee-house.

'Interests started with theoretical physics, shifted to biochemistry, psychology, poetry, economics, magic, exchange functions, patterns of existence, emotional flow, individual and group ecology. Believe that matter is conscious, things will always be the same as they always were, everything will work out as it should, and in you.'

JOEL SLOMAN

'Born in Brooklyn, June 23, 1943. Public schools in Brooklyn and City College. No degree. Readings at Guggenheim, Poetry Center, St. Mark's, as well as colleges and N.Y. public schools. Worked at Poetry Project, St. Mark's. Edited first couple of issues of *The World.* Served as juror.

Attended juvenile delinquency conference in Washington. Voted in last three elections. Leaving for Europe to write a novel.'

Virgil's Machines. New York: W. W. Norton & Co., 1966.

LYNN STRONGIN

'I was born in N.Y.C., 1939, grew up in & around N.Y., went to Hunter College where I gave my first readings of my poetry, then over WBAI. Now I live on the West Coast & have participated in readings with some of the poets here. I will have poems published soon in: *The Goliards, Bay Podium,* & *Galley Sail Review.* Have taught college in N.Y. & in California.'

JOHN UNTERECKER

'John Unterecker (born Buffalo, New York, on December 14, 1922) has worked as night watchman, college professor, radio announcer, factory worker, biographer, actor, literary critic, file clerk, and poet. He has collaborated with the artist George Weinheimer on a book for children and has edited a group of hitherto unpublished Yeats letters for Dolmen Press in Dublin. His best work, he feels, is his poetry.

'As an avocation, he grows rhododendron and some of the rarer gesneriads. His wife, Ann, is a professional musician. They live in a white house that is surrounded by fruit trees and smog.'

Voyager: The Life of Hart Crane. New York: Farrar, Straus & Giroux.
A Reader's Guide to W. B. Yeats. New York: Noonday Press, 1959.
Lawrence Durrell. New York: Columbia University Press, 1964.
The Dreaming Zoo. New York: Henry Z. Walk, Inc., 1965.

JOHN STEVENS WADE

'Born: Smithfield, Maine, 1928. Education: Maine schools, U.S. Army, Connecticut State College. Former hotel manager, public relations assistant, mail carrier, bank teller, carpenter, town official, and auditor. Married Stella Taschlicky in 1954. Two children. Began writing poetry regularly in 1956. Built a cottage in Maine in 1959 and lived partly under the influence of "Walden" for five years. Moved to Holland in 1964, returned to Maine for a year, and presently lives in Headford, Ireland.'

NANCY WILLARD

'Born June 26, 1936. B.A., Ph.D., University of
    Michigan, M.A. Stanford.
Teaching at Vassar.
Married, to Eric Lindbloom.'

In His Country. Ann Arbor: University of Michigan New Poets
    Series, 1966.
Skin of Grace. Columbia, Missouri: University of Missouri Press,
    1967.

KEITH WILSON

'Born December 26, 1927, in Clovis, New Mexico. Grew up in New Mexico and the Southwest, punching cows, digging ditches, working on farms and ranches. Attended 15 different grammar schools and 3 high schools. . . . Received appointment to the United States Naval Academy in 1945 and graduated from there in the Class of 1950. Next four years spent at sea, mainly in Korea (five battle stars). . . . Went to University of New Mexico to receive a Master's degree in literature in 1956. Since then has taught mainly writing at various universities. . . . Now an assistant professor of English at New Mexico State University, Las Cruces, New Mexico. Married, 1958, to Heloise Brigham.'

> *Sketches for a New Mexico Hill Town.* Milwaukee, Oregon: Presna de Lagar/WINE PRESS, 1966.
> *The Old Car & Other Black Poems.* Seattle: Grande Ronde Press, 1967.
> *Lion's Gate.* New York: Grove Press, 1968.

JAY WRIGHT

'I was born in Albuquerque, New Mexico, on May 25, 1935. I grew up in San Pedro, California, knocked around as a professional baseball player for a couple of years and went into the army. I took a B.A. from the University of California at Berkeley, attended Union Theological Seminary in New York . . . for about four months, went to Rutgers University in New Brunswick and got my M.A. in Comparative Literature. I wrote my first play (my first anything) around the age of twenty-five or twenty-six, and have only been writing seriously for three years or so. Anything of mine that anyone shows me from the period before that draws my wrath. I've had two short plays produced; one at the Playwrights' Workshop on the Berkeley campus, one at the Exodus Coffee Shop in San Pedro. . . . I'm trying to finish up two long plays now. I have an unpublished book of poems, *Idiotic and Politic: Preliminary Dances.* . . . I'll have poems in future issues of *The Nation, Poetry Review, Negro Digest* and *Hiram Poetry Review,* as well as *The Poetry of the Negro* and an anthology of Black writing edited by LeRoi Jones and Larry Neal for Morrow.'